Workbook

Lynne Evans

Business
Partner

B1+

T0345778

Contents

1 ▶ Organisation

Vocabulary   Roles and responsibilities

1 Choose the correct option in italics.

1 The *heads / base* of departments must attend the meeting arranged for 4.30 p.m.

2 Fabio will *make sure / take care* of all the catering arrangements for your client meeting.

3 If you can multitask, you shouldn't have a problem *involving / running* this department.

4 As from today I *lead / report* to the Sales Director.

5 Stephan is *responsible / coordinates* for all the company's advertising.

6 If you love watching sports, you should consider a career as a sports *journalist / trainer* reporting on sporting events.

7 We need to hire a(n) *actor / camera operator* to read the script in a convincing way.

2 Choose the correct option to complete the sentences.

1 I need you to _____ that everything runs smoothly at the conference.

  a be responsible   **b** make sure   **c** work closely

2 Sara should _____ the Marketing Manager rather than work alone.

  a lead   **b** take care of   **c** coordinate with

3 Toni is _____ of this team as of today.

  a looking after   **b** making sure   **c** in charge

4 The _____ will make sure that we have everything we need for the meeting.

  a hotel manager   **b** journalist   **c** sports trainer

5 You have to _____ to your line manager, Ms Gibrain.

  a work closely   **b** report   **c** coordinate

6 Ms Schmidt is the _____ of the Sales Department.

  a camera operator   **b** head   **c** role

3 Complete the missing letters to form words and complete the sentences.

1 B_ _ _ a_c_ _ _y is a system that has a lot of rules.

2 She started at the bottom and worked her way up the h_ _ _ _a_ _h_.

3 If Audric works hard, he will get a p_ _ _o_ _ _n, I think.

4 This is a very i_ _o_ _t _v_ idea and very creative, too.

5 It's time the company moved out of its headquarters and d_ _ _n_ _a_ _s_d.

6 The company decided to go against the trend and c_ _t_ _l_ _e its operations.

Grammar Future forms

1 Match the sentences to the uses.

1 a personal intention ____ ____

2 a plan/arrangement ____ ____

3 a prediction ____ ____

4 a scheduled event ____ ____

a It's going to be an informative talk, I'm sure.

b Carlotta is speaking at the conference.

c I'm sure that you are all going to do your best to make this a success.

d I'm meeting the Sales Director on Friday.

e I'm going on holiday next week.

f Marcelina is going to be out of the office until Thursday next week.

g Freidrick is going to oversee the expansion himself.

h Toni will give the presentation tomorrow.

2 Put the words in the correct order to complete the sentences.

1 Tuesday / in / won't / be / I / on / the / office

_____

2 later / are / meeting / going / you / to / the / ?

_____

3 next / we're / conference / visiting / centre / week / the

_____

4 Lamar / promotion / I / is / get / soon / to / going / think / a

_____

5 Monday / we / have / leave / early / to / on / don't

_____

6 weather / flight / won't / our / leave / on time / in / this

_____

7 Faiza / chair / on / will / the / Thursday / meeting

_____

8 conference / isn't / to / going / until / the / finish / late

_____

3 Complete the email with the correct form of the verbs in brackets.

Hi Kim,

Carla ¹_____ (go) to the conference in Stockholm with Juan, who ²_____ (drive) there. However, I ³_____ (have) an appointment in the morning, so I'm going to drive down afterwards. Unfortunately, the traffic ⁴_____ (be) heavy around lunchtime, but I hope to get there by 12.30 p.m. The first seminar ⁵_____ (start) at 1 p.m. so that should be fine.

⁶_____ (you/come) with me or Carla? We ⁷_____ (have) a meeting in-house in the afternoon, so you can let me know then.

See you soon,

Christoph

Reading

Médecins Sans Frontières

The international non-governmental organisation (NGO), Médecins Sans Frontières (MSF), or Doctors without Borders, was founded in 1971. Its purpose was to help people who needed medical aid following natural disasters, or political violence and wars.

In the beginning, there were only thirteen doctors and journalists. Since then it has expanded dramatically and has offices all over the world. By 1972 there were 300 volunteers, including the thirteen original founders. In that year, MSF's first task was to help people in Managua, the capital city of Nicaragua, after an earthquake. Between 10,000 and 30,000 people died. In 1974, staff went to Honduras after Hurricane Fifi and the flooding that followed. The following year MSF assisted in its first refugee crisis, helping Cambodians who had fled their country.

During the 70s, there were problems for the MSF staff on the ground; there was little preparation before staff set off on a mission; doctors had little support and supply lines were not reliable. At that time, there were no humanitarian logisticians, so ports and airports became blocked because of aid packages that had been sent from all over the world.

Now things have changed. The organisation employs more than 36,000 people around the world. These people support the medical professionals and include logisticians, heads of fundraising, coordinators, managers and accountants. There are also many thousands of volunteers.

All operation bases need a manager and other staff to raise funds and plan how to deliver aid where it is needed. The manager has to resolve problems, as well as decide on and implement fund-raising strategies. He or she must also ensure that projects don't go over budget.

NGO accountants assist the manager with the financial side of the operation. They have to work out the budget, make sure that staff are paid, pay bills and train local staff to control their own budgets. The manager and coordinator train volunteers to do their jobs. The coordinator develops and implements training programmes and is responsible for making travel arrangements and arranging meetings.

The organisation is continuing its work, helping sick and distressed people wherever help is needed.

1 **Read the article and decide if the statements are *true* (T) or *false* (F).**

1 MSF started in 1972. ____

2 The organisation was started by thirteen doctors and journalists. ____

3 It first helped refugees in 1974. ____

4 In MSF's first few years there were logistical problems. ____

5 MSF only employs medical personnel. ____

6 The manager can give permission for a project to exceed its budget. ____

7 The accountant is solely responsible for making sure all staff receive training. ____

2 **Read the article again and choose the correct option.**

1 In which year did MSF start delivering aid?

    a 1971   **b** 1972   **c** 1974   **d** 1975

2 Where did MSF <u>not</u> work?

    a Honduras   **b** Cambodia   **c** Nicaragua   **d** Managua

3 Which job title was notably absent during the first refugee crisis?

    a manager   **b** coordinator   **c** accountant   **d** logistician

4 Whose responsibility is it to train local volunteers?

    a manager and accountant   **c** coordinator

    b manager and coordinator   **d** manager

5 Who is responsible for staff training programmes?

    a manager and coordinator   **c** accountant

    b accountant and manager   **d** coordinator

6 Whose job is it to buy flight tickets?

    a manager   **b** coordinator   **c** accountant   **d** logistician

3 **What is the purpose of the article?**

a To inform **b** To entertain **c** To persuade

Functional language

Greetings, introductions and goodbyes

1 **Match a question or expression (1–7) with a response (a–g).**

1 Hello. I'm Nathan Roberts.

2 How's it going?

3 Can I get you anything to drink?

4 Everything's fine. Good trip?

5 So, first time in Shanghai?

6 Let's meet the others.

7 Do you know James?

a A bit of a delay on the trains today.

b A bit. I met him in Paris a few months ago.

c Not bad, not bad. How about you?

d Hi, Nathan. Nice to finally meet you in person.

e Great! Can't wait!

f A coffee, please.

g No, I was here last year.

Asking and answering questions in first meetings

2 **Complete the conversation with the questions in the box. There are two extra sentences.**

> do you report to Charu Patel   when did you join the company   can I take your coat
> did you have a good trip   do you work with Beena   can I get you something to drink
> where are you based   can I order you a taxi   are you free for dinner this evening
> is it your first time in the Mexico office

A: Hello, nice to meet you.

B: You too.

A: ¹_____?

B: That would be great, thanks.

A: Please, sit down. ²_____?

B: A glass of water, please.

A: So, ³_____?

B: No, I was here two years ago, actually.

A: Really? ⁴_____?

B: About six years ago.

A: ⁵_____?

B: In Delhi at the moment, but I was in Dubai for a long time.

A: In Delhi? ⁶_____?

B: Yes, I do. Do you know her?

A: Yes, we worked together on a project in Frankfurt.
So, ⁷_____?

B: No, David Cope in Dubai is still my manager.

A: OK. ⁸_____?

B: Not today. Are you free tomorrow?

Writing Emails – Organising information

1 Complete the letter with the words in the box.

questions further hesitate Madam after sincerely inform

Dear Sir / [1] _____ ,

I am writing to [2] _____ you of where we are in the process of selling your house.
[3] _____ to our conversation, I confirm that the contract for the sale of your house has been sent to the buyers. We expect the signed contract to be returned by the end of the week.
[4] _____ that, you will need to vacate the property and hand over the keys by Saturday 28th. Please do not [5] _____ to contact me if you have any
[6] _____ regarding the sale.

Yours [7] _____ ,

Daniel Marston

2 Amalia is writing to her manager, Eleni, to ask questions about a conference. Put the paragraphs in the correct order.

To:	Eleni Papageorgiou
From:	Amalia Esposito
Subject:	Digital Marketing conference

Hi Eleni,

1 ____ (A) Next, are we going by train or are we car-sharing, please?

2 ____ (B) First of all, could you let me know how many of my colleagues are going to the conference?

3 ____ (C) I hope everything goes well, and that there will be information that we can apply to our own operation.

4 ____ (D) Sorry to bother you, but I have a few questions about the upcoming conference on Digital Marketing.

5 ____ (E) Finally, can you tell me which workshops you would like me to prioritise, as there are several scheduled for the same time.

Best wishes,

Amalia

3 Write a reply of about 80 words to the email in Exercise 2.

• Begin and end appropriately.

• Say why you are writing.

• Order the information (in the order of the questions).

• Use the Present Simple and Present Continuous where possible.

2 ▶ Brands

Vocabulary Marketing and brands

1 Choose the correct option in italics.

1 Market research suggests that we need to change our *image / growth / base* to appeal to younger customers.

2 Although we have built up an excellent *history / base / market* of clients, we still need to attract new accounts.

3 Our fast *history / growth / placement* means that we have a high profile in the industry.

4 The interactive marketing campaign has been successful as customer *engagement / awareness / image* has increased dramatically.

5 Rather than take a cautious *business / image / approach*, we need to be bold and innovative.

6 The bank has refused our request for a further overdraft because of our bad repayment *image / history / base*.

7 Brand stretching would help us *develop / venture / approach* into new markets.

8 Older consumers tend to be *loyal / interactive / careful* to brands, whereas younger ones are more likely to switch.

2 Complete the words. Use the definitions to help you.

1 b_____ s_____ when a company starts to use an existing brand name on another different type of product, hoping that people will buy it because they recognise the name

2 c_____ b_____ the part of the company that makes the most money and that is considered to be its most important and central one

3 d_____ to make something appear less important or desirable

4 p_____ p_____ a form of advertising in which a company arranges for its goods to appear in a television programme or film

5 l_____ the quality of remaining faithful to a person, product, company, etc.

6 u_____-_____ highly expensive and exclusive

7 i_____ m_____ a strategy that uses two-way communication channels to allow consumers to connect with a company directly

3 Complete the sentences using the words and phrases from Exercise 2.

1 One of the most famous examples of _____ _____ are the Aston Martin cars in the James Bond films.

2 Bulgari's move from jewellery into the hotel business is an interesting case of _____ _____.

3 A successful example of _____ _____ is Amazon's 'suggested reading' for customers which is based on the books they have bought in the past.

4 Nike's _____ _____ is making sports shoes.

5 Good copies of Gucci bags can _____ the original product.

6 Department stores encourage customer _____ by offering discount store cards.

7 Cartier and Hermès are examples of _____ _____ brands.

Grammar Connectors

1 Choose the correct option.

1 *For instance / First of all*, I want to welcome everyone to the opening of our new store.

2 We've had a few setbacks *and / but* now we're on track to complete the project on schedule.

3 There are several decisions to make concerning the way forward. *However / For example*, should we buy new software or update what we have?

4 The new product lines from Bulgari are elegant *but / and* ultra-stylish.

5 *In addition / Although* Chinese products were once regarded as cheap and even dangerous, they have changed dramatically over the years.

6 We should look into the possibility of expanding our operations *as well as / to start with* finding more markets in Asia.

7 *For instance / In addition* to stocking luxury brands, we also have a huge range of affordable products.

8 I want to congratulate you all on our success so far, *however / also*, we have a long way to go. Keep up the good work!

2 Match 1–8 with a–h to complete the sentences.

1 We need to stop fake luxury goods being sold on the streets,

2 Our sales figures were better last year,

3 We mustn't forget to market the non-luxury items

4 We need to attract new customers

5 We did not achieve our sales target this quarter,

6 Let's consider our options to start with

7 Our profit margins are good,

8 I'd just like to say,

a however, we did not quite meet our sales target.

b but it is difficult to know how to do this.

c and then we can make some decisions.

d while keeping our existing ones.

e although we've all worked very hard.

f in addition to my earlier remarks, that you have worked well as a team.

g when we were using traditional forms of advertising.

h as well as our designer brands.

3 Choose the correct option.

1 Our sales figures are good,
  a but we can't relax yet.
  b although, we can now take it easy.

2 Our luxury brands are selling well,
  a although the cheaper ranges aren't.
  b for example, the cheaper ranges aren't.

3 We need to improve our image,
  a although we need to explore new markets.
  b also we need to expand our market.

4 We need more funding for this project,
  a for instance, we can continue.
  b then we can move on.

5 Right, let's begin.
  a For instance, can we have some suggestions.
  b First of all, I'd like some suggestions.

6 We now have the results of our survey.
  a Recently, they were as predicted.
  b Although, unfortunately they were as we predicted.

7 Our upcoming conference should be well-attended,
  a but we still need to advertise it online.
  b for example, we need to advertise it online.

8 Our Bulgari range is selling very well.
  a Such as are our cheaper ranges.
  b In addition, so are our cheaper products.

Listening

1 🔊 2.01 **Listen to a woman talking about her company on the radio. Decide if the statements are *true* (T) or *false* (F).**

1 Cynthia is used to being on the radio. ＿＿＿＿

2 Her company exclusively makes woollen clothing. ＿＿＿＿

3 The business developed from her hobby. ＿＿＿＿

4 At first the clothes were sold only in local shops. ＿＿＿＿

5 Cynthia took a course in clothing design. ＿＿＿＿

6 Product placement boosted sales. ＿＿＿＿

7 The jumpers are still hand-knitted. ＿＿＿＿

8 Cynthia doesn't want anything to do with woolly clothes in her retirement. ＿＿＿＿

2 **Listen again and choose the correct option.**

1 Why is the company name not really appropriate now?

    a None of the clothes are made from wool.

    b The clothes are made from several different materials.

    c Most of the clothes are made from cotton.

    d The clothes are for all seasons.

2 How did Cynthia feel about her early business?

    a She was surprised at its success.

    b She enjoyed her popularity.

    c She was overwhelmed by the amount of orders she was receiving.

    d She was disappointed.

3 The Woolly brand sells itself because

    a the garments are expensive.

    b the garments are unique.

    c the garments are only made from good quality materials.

    d a well-known celebrity advertises them.

4 Which country outside Britain did she first sell her clothes to?

    a France

    b Germany

    c USA

    d Denmark

5 When did she first realise the importance of brand loyalty?

    a From the beginning.

    b When she got mail from different countries.

    c When clients began to order tops in advance.

    d When customers wrote to her personally.

6 Now her problem is that

    a she doesn't speak any Asian languages.

    b she needs to employ more people.

    c she needs to find reliable sales people.

    d she needs a translating program for Asian languages.

7 What is her main focus for the future?

    a to work on new designs and materials

    b to expand into warmer markets

    c to retire

    d to learn another language quickly

3 **Choose the best title for the radio programme.**

a Five rules for growing a business

b Learning business the hard way

c Woolly – a success story

Functional language

Giving and responding to advice

1 Complete the sentences with the words in the box.

| would   able   afraid   should   important   tried |

1 Have you _____ talking to them about it?

2 Don't be _____ to ask your manager for help.

3 I think it's _____ for us to find a solution today.

4 Maybe it _____ be better for us to delay the project for a month.

5 Customer service _____ be the company's main focus.

6 You need to be _____ to prioritise your work on your own.

2 Choose the correct form of the verb to complete the sentences.

1 Why don't you *talk / talking* to your line manager?

2 Maybe it would be better *take / to take* a few days off.

3 Have you tried *to work / working* at home?

4 Don't be afraid *giving / to give* your real reason.

5 Maybe you should *do / doing* some more training.

6 You need *rescheduling / to reschedule* your team meetings.

7 I think it's important for you *spend / to spend* more time with your team.

Signposting in presentations

3 Match 1–6 with a–f to complete the sentences.

1 Please feel

2 There's one important point I'd like to

3 Thank you for listening to me. I will now hand

4 Welcome everyone. Let's begin

5 If you can all take

6 I don't have anything else to say so I

a will close there.

b over to Anna.

c free to ask any questions.

d with the most important problem first.

e make about the company.

f a look at page 36.

Writing Formal and semi-formal emails

1 Put letters in brackets in the correct order to complete the email.

To: Victor Kreuz

From: Luca Schmidt

Dear Mr Kreuz,

We are [1]_____ (ddgteihel) to announce that we are opening our new conference facilities on 28th February. The opening ceremony will be [2]_____ (dhle) in the main auditorium on the first floor, at 5.30 p.m. As a preferred client, you and your partner are [3]_____ (vindite) to attend.

The conference centre was designed by Cora Bhatti in [4]_____ (llcooaibootnra) with Ashaf Tahir.

Dinner will be served at 7 p.m.

Please [5]_____ (mncofri) your attendance by 1st February and remember to bring this invitation with you to gain admittance to the venue.

We very much look [6]_____ (wdrfoar) to seeing you at this event.

Kind [7]_____ (gredars),
Luca Schmidt

2 Complete the email declining the invitation in Exercise 1 with the words and phrases in the box.

I'm afraid   be unable   best regards   Thank you   I hope   the invitation

To: Luca Schmidt

From: Victor Kreuz

Dear Mr Schmidt,

[1]_____ very much for [2]_____ to the opening ceremony for your new conference facilities. [3]_____ that my wife and I will [4]_____ to attend due to a prior engagement.

[5]_____ that you have a very successful opening and look forward to meeting you again in the near future.

With [6]_____,
Victor Kreuz

3 Write a reply of about 80 words to the email in Exercise 1.

- Decide whether to write a formal or semi-formal email.
- Open and close an email appropriately.
- Thank Mr Schmidt for the invitation.
- Accept the invitation.

3 ⟩ Job-hunting

Vocabulary Getting a job

1 **Complete the text with the words in the box.**

| be of value to   clichéd   come across well   employers   jobseekers   stand out from |

There are a lot of candidates for the manager's job. People know we're good
¹_____ and that's why so many ²_____ have applied. We will
be looking for people who ³_____ the crowd and who will
⁴_____ our company. We select candidates who ⁵_____ in
their interviews. We are not looking for ⁶_____ expressions in the CVs,
but for real creativity.

2 **Put the words in brackets in the correct form.**

1 Why not apply for an _____ (*intern*) to get work experience?

2 This _____ (*employ*) likes to hire people without much experience.

3 We have to be better than the _____ (*compete*) if our business is to succeed.

4 These days _____ (*job*) have to have more than a university degree to get a job.

5 You need to have good _____ (*communicate*) skills in order to do well in interviews.

6 A self-starter has to have the _____ (*motivate*) to succeed.

3 **Find the words in the wordsearch. Use the definitions to help you.**

1 someone in a company who is involved in employing new staff

2 used to describe a person, plan, etc. that can change or be changed easily to suit any new situation

3 the combination of qualities that makes someone a particular type of person

4 formal word for 'job'

5 a job that lasts for a short time that someone, especially a student, does in order to gain experience

6 an ability to do something well, especially because you have learned and practised it

F	H	F	C	F	K	M	V	A	X
M	J	S	H	J	H	P	F	D	E
S	O	A	A	D	U	O	L	F	T
E	P	C	R	E	P	F	E	G	Y
R	L	B	A	B	O	V	X	K	R
T	K	U	C	N	S	K	I	L	L
K	E	I	T	M	I	L	B	L	N
L	E	M	E	V	T	C	L	S	A
R	E	C	R	U	I	T	E	R	Y
O	T	W	K	E	O	D	Z	O	L
I	N	T	E	R	N	S	H	I	P

Grammar Indirect questions

1A Decide if these are *direct* (D) or *indirect* (I) questions.

1 Are you prepared to move if you get this job? ____

2 Could you tell me what you liked the most about your last job? ____

3 Why did you apply for this job? ____

4 I'd like to know if you've worked abroad. ____

5 How did you find out about this position? ____

6 Why did you leave your last job? ____

7 Can you tell me who you admire most in your present company? ____

8 I'd like to know what you think your main weakness is. ____

B Now change the direct questions from Exercise 4A to indirect questions and the indirect questions to direct questions. Use the prompts.

1 _____ (like to know)

2 _____ (what)

3 _____ (can)

4 _____ (have)

5 _____ (could)

6 _____ (like to know)

7 _____ (who)

8 _____ (what)

2 Put the words into the correct order to make indirect questions.

1 yourself / tell / more / a / about / you / could / me / little

_____

2 last / how / I'd like / you / worked for / employer / many years / to know / your

_____

3 job / why / left / tell / previous / me / your / you / please

_____

4 I'd / to / like / know more / responsibilities / about / your / last / job / in / your

_____

5 I / an internship / if you / would / need / applying / like / for / consider / to / ask

_____

6 ambitions / I / if / could / wonder / you / more / about / say / your

_____

7 job / emigrate / the / for / me / could / you'd / tell / you / if

_____

8 experience / I'd / to / about / your / like / tell / you / me / leadership

_____

Reading

1 Read the article below and label the paragraphs (1–5) with the correct heading (a–f).

a Tailor your CV

b Show some enthusiasm

c Do your research

d Prepare for the interview

e Overcoming fears

f Tell the truth

2 Choose the correct option.

1 Why doesn't careers advice always help people find work?

a Because it doesn't focus on how to look for a job.

b Because people don't always follow the advice.

c Because it only focuses on practicalities.

2 Where should you look for jobs, according to the text?

a In print newspapers.

b Online.

c In an agency.

3 Why don't some suitably qualified people get an interview?

a Because they are too old.

b Because they play up their skills.

c Because their curriculum vitae is not matched to the job.

4 What should you do before an interview?

a Research the company.

b Send a letter to the company.

c Visit the company.

5 What should you avoid focusing on in your interview questions?

a Details of the new role.

b Pay and holidays.

c Other applicants.

6 How can you show you have prepared for an interview?

a By preparing relevant questions.

b By buying new clothes.

c By being eager.

7 Why must you always tell the truth?

a Because it is illegal to tell lies in an interview.

b Because you can't delete private information online.

c Because the company will find out if you don't.

Advice for Jobseekers

1 _____

It can be quite scary when it comes to marketing yourself. Although you may have had careers advice, this probably focused on which career is most suited to your skills and qualities rather than on the practicalities of looking for a job. However, you will be pleased to know there are several useful tips for jobseekers to help them get that all-important position.

2 _____

First of all, you will need to search online newspapers and job sites for suitable openings. When you find a position to apply for, you have to mould your experience to fit the job description. Many people don't get interviews because their curriculum vitae is not directly relevant to the job. Play up the skills you have that are needed for the job.

3 _____

Find out as much as you can about the company you are applying to. Look at their website and find out more about what the company does and the current issues it is facing. If you know someone who already works for the company, ask how they feel about their job.

4 _____

Think about the questions you could ask in your interview. Interviewees are always asked if they have any questions and these should not just be about pay and holidays. You need to show that you are eager to work for that company in particular and are interested in it. Your questions should demonstrate that you have thought about your interview. This will impress the interviewers who will look more favourably on you than on other candidates for the job who are not as well prepared. You need to stand out from all the other applicants.

5 _____

Don't lie. Employers will check. These days they may even look at social media accounts. You might want to delete anything they might consider inappropriate. Don't neglect to do this.

6 _____

Finally, the more you can demonstrate how eager you are based on the research you have done and the questions you have prepared, the better your chances of landing the job you want.

Functional language

Active listening

1 **Match the sentences to the uses.**

Clarifying/Exploring	____	____
Summarising/Paraphrasing	____	____
Checking understanding	____	____
Correcting	____	____
Giving feedback	____	____

1 So, it's important for you to sell some shares, but still keep control of the company. Right?

2 OK, that's really useful to know.

3 How would you improve our customer service?

4 Sorry, that's not what I was trying to say.

5 OK, why don't you tell me when the company started losing money?

6 I can see you are finding it difficult.

7 I'm not clear about what the actual problem is.

8 No, that's not what we agreed.

9 What do you mean by 'needing more investment'?

10 So, you aren't interested in selling your share of the business?

Useful phrases for candidates

2 **Match 1–6 with a–f to complete the sentences.**

1	When can I expect	**a**	to talking to you about this role.
2	There are two ways	**b**	to answer your question.
3	Thank you very much for taking	**c**	a normal day is like?
4	I'm looking forward	**d**	the time to talk to me today.
5	It's good you	**e**	to hear from you?
6	Could you tell me what	**f**	asked that.

3 **Complete the conversations with the sentences in the box.**

> I look forward to hearing from you.   That's a good question.
> Can I speak to some of the people I would be working with?
> Thank you for your time today.   I haven't had that exact experience.
> Could you tell me more about the training programme?

1 C: _____

    I: Thank you for coming at such short notice.

2 C: _____

    I: Well, we encourage all our staff members to continue developing their skills.

3 I: Have you ever had to ask a customer to leave?

    C: _____

4 C: _____

    I: Yes, of course. I will introduce you shortly.

5 I: We will be in touch soon.

    C: _____

6 I: Why do you think you are the right person for this role?

    C: _____

Writing Covering letter

1 **Complete the covering letter with the words and phrases in the box.**

advertised asset confident degree enclosed experience grateful vacancy

Dear Ms Arshad,
Re: Position of Sales Assistant

I am writing to apply for the ¹_____ of sales assistant as ²_____ on the Careers website last week. Please find ³_____ my curriculum vitae for your information. As you will see from my CV, I have a first-class ⁴_____ in Sales and feel that I would be a suitable fit for your company. I have been working in a similar position for two years, where I have developed my skills and expertise. I am a valued member of the sales team, I work hard to make sure that I am fully up to date with current trends in the sales sector and I consistently achieve my sales targets in my current position. I am now ready to take the next step in my career and I am ⁵_____ that my ⁶_____ would be a(n) ⁷_____ to your company. I would be ⁸_____ to have the opportunity to attend an interview to find out more about the role and demonstrate my skills.

Yours sincerely,
Andrea Buxton

2 **Read the job advert and write a covering letter applying for the job in around 180 words. Include the following:**

- State which job you are applying for and where you saw the advert.
- Give your reasons for applying for the job.
- Say why you think you would be the best candidate for the job.
- Begin and end the letter appropriately.

Marketing manager required

Are you competitive? Do you have a degree in marketing? Are you looking for a position within a market leader? Are you willing to travel?

You will be responsible for our European project. You must be a team player but also be able to lead a strong dynamic team with little support. Experience is a must. A second language is desirable.

Surfing Technologies are based in Sydney and we have a proven track record in offering our services.

If you think you have the necessary skills and are passionate about your career, please send your CV with a covering letter to Head of Resources at hr@marketingfirst.com.

Successful candidates will be called to interview.

Vocabulary   Business strategy collocations

1 **Put the letters in brackets in the correct order to complete the sentences.**

1 In 2010 Kraft made a successful _____ (ktaoerve) bid for Cadbury.

2 We shouldn't miss the _____ (potporuniiest) that present themselves.

3 Our new _____ (docprut) line is selling well.

4 We must develop new _____ (gasterties) to attract clients.

5 Kraft Heinz is a _____ (jamor) player in the food industry.

2 **Choose the correct option.**

1 Our ____ margins are not as good as they could be.

  a development   **b** profit   **c** innovation   **d** strategy

2 Our travel budget must be suspended if we are going to make a ____ this year.

  a cost   **b** profit   **c** margin   **d** opportunity

3 It is necessary to ____ this problem immediately.

  a take   **b** make   **c** miss   **d** solve

4 Has anyone come up with a ____ for our next advertising campaign yet?

  a plan   **b** problem   **c** risk   **d** cost

5 If we come across problems, they will have to be ____.

  a tackled   **b** taken   **c** missed   **d** planned

Word building – verbs, nouns and adjectives

3 **Use the clues to complete the crossword.**

Across

4 to obtain something by buying it or being given it

5 to do what you tried or wanted to do

7 the joining together of two or more companies or organisations to form one larger one

9 a lack of success in achieving or doing something

Down

1 to become larger in size, number, or amount, or to make something become larger

2 making money, not losing (for a business or company)

3 the process of gradually becoming bigger, better, stronger or more advanced

6 an increase in amount, number or size

8 involving a possibility that something bad will happen

Grammar Modal verbs

1 Rewrite the sentences using the correct modal verbs.

1 Choose a personal password that's easy to remember. (good idea)

You _____ choose a personal password that's easy to remember.

2 Log off at the end of the day. (necessary)

You _____ log off at the end of the day.

3 Don't back up your files. (not necessary)

You _____ back up your files.

4 Don't give anyone the password to the company system. (not allowed)

You _____ give anyone the password to the company system.

5 Keep your desktop tidy. (good idea)

You _____ keep your desktop tidy.

6 Use the company content management system. (necessary)

You _____ use the company content management system.

7 Don't download software from the internet. (not allowed)

You _____ download software from the internet.

8 Don't run any security checks. They're done automatically. (not necessary)

You _____ run any security checks.

2 Choose the correct option in italics.

1 We'll *have to / should* move quickly if we are to close this deal.

2 You really *should / don't have to* do everything. Learn to delegate.

3 Abida *must / shouldn't* have total responsibility for the project; she doesn't have enough experience.

4 You really *don't have to / mustn't* take new stationery without signing for it.

5 I think you *should / must* check before the meeting that your Skype connection works.

6 We'll *have to / should* make a decision by the end of this week.

7 I think you *must / should* check the figures again before you give the presentation.

8 You really *mustn't / shouldn't* work in your lunch hour. It isn't allowed.

3 Complete the sentences with the correct form of the words in the box. Use some of the words more than once.

have to   must   should

1 You _____ report everything that was said, just give me an outline.

2 Jamil _____ complete his tax return before the deadline.

3 He will _____ visit the client and try to save the account.

4 You _____ expect to know everything. You're still new here.

5 I am expected at the meeting in five minutes, so I will _____ go now.

6 We _____ tell her it was our mistake. We don't have a choice!

7 We _____ wait a few more minutes before we start the meeting.

8 You _____ ask a customer to leave unless it's absolutely necessary.

Reading

1 Complete the text with these sentences.

A There are different ways a company can create this value through innovative technology, efficient supply chains and brands that take a long time to cultivate.

B The important thing is to identify one's target market.

C President Shigeru Yamashita says the key to success is the company's focus on babies up to 18 months old.

D They are not strategy, either.

E It is a relatively small company, with sales of less than 100 billion yen ($876 million).

F One definition of strategy is that it is a way of creating unique value.

2 Read the text again and decide if these sentences are *true* (T) or *false* (F).

1 There is some confusion about what exactly business strategy is. ____

2 A company should aim at providing value for money. ____

3 Above all, managers should have a plan for making a company profitable. ____

4 Pigeon does not make much profit, given its size. ____

5 The reason for Pigeon's recent success is that it sells to international markets. ____

6 The company grew because it learned from its mistakes. ____

3 What is the article mainly about?

a The market for baby products in Japan.

b The focus on sales and profits in business.

c The importance of providing what customers really need.

CREATING UNIQUE VALUE
is the essence of business strategy

TOKYO

Managers often talk about business strategy, but the term is somewhat mysterious.

Companies set sales and profit targets in their midterm business plans, but these are not strategy. Many tend to rely on organisational reforms to help them achieve their goals, but these are just a means to an end. ¹____

²____ If a company can outdo the competition and provide unique value to its customers, it can both make money and contribute to society.

³____ But managers' biggest responsibility is to draw up a blueprint for building a distinct corporate identity.

Japanese baby goods maker Pigeon offers a good example. ⁴____ But its operating margin of over 15% is exceptionally high among Japanese manufacturers.

⁵____ Feeding children at this age is something all parents think about and high-quality baby bottles sell well in any country.

Although the number of babies in Japan is falling, Pigeon's sales have risen by about 50% over the past five years, thanks to rapid growth overseas.

Some of the company's products are a big hit. The company has also developed a solid brand and distribution network in China by partnering with well-known hospitals to set up in-house child care consultation rooms.

⁶____The market for baby clothes is much bigger than that for baby bottles, but Pigeon has decided not to expand into that market because it would be difficult for it to stand out from the crowd through technology in the clothing business, and to meet the demands of a different market. Despite these insights, Yamashita acknowledged that he did not have a clear strategy from the outset. 'We owe our success to many failures in the past,' Yamashita said. 'It is a continuing process of trial and error.'

Functional language

Offering and asking for help

1 Complete the conversations with the words in the box.

> hand   mind   anything   would   let   fine   like   could   offering   appreciate

1 A: Is there _____ I can do to help?

  B: No, thanks. I'm _____.

2 A: Need a _____ with anything?

  B: Yeah. _____ you grab those files for me?

3 A: _____ you like me to do anything?

  B: Thanks for _____ but I think I'll be OK.

4 A: _____ me give you a hand with that projector.

  B: Thanks. I _____ it.

5 A: I'd _____ to help. What can I do?

  B: Would you _____ helping me with this box?

Leading and participating in problem-solving meetings

2 Complete the phrases with the words in the box.

> pick up   take this on   exactly   building on   doable   not sure   how about   sense

Clarifying the problem	Can you explain again what the problem is, [1] _____?
Suggesting a solution	[2] _____ asking Simon to do it? He has the experience.
Building on others' ideas	To [3] _____ on what Maria said, why don't we employ more staff? Just [4] _____ Chan's idea, I think we should recruit someone who has recently qualified.
Agreeing	I think it's a great idea; simple and [5] _____. I think that makes a lot of [6] _____.
Disagreeing	I'm [7] _____ how that would work, exactly.
Offering to help	Shall I [8] _____, or do you have time to do it?

Writing   Reporting reasons and results

1   Complete the report with the words in the box.

as a result   because   due   has led   have resulted in   in order to   resulting in   so

---

Report on Current Problems

Our retail company has faced considerable problems this year.
This report aims to outline the main ones.

Main Problems and Reasons

The main problem affects businesses across the country. [1]_____ to high unemployment, people have less disposable income to spend.

As well as this, manufacturing costs have increased. This [2]_____ to a fall in profit margins. Up until now we have tried not to pass on the additional costs to our customers. However, we will have to raise our prices if we are to stay in business. Instead we reduced our range of products, [3]_____ we lost customers.
If we have fewer customers, our sales figures will fall even further. If we lose customers, we will need to cut staff.

New government taxes are making it difficult for businesses, too. The new business rates for properties [4]_____ a number of shop closures up and down the country.

A new discount chain began operations at the beginning of the year.
[5]_____ , sales dropped [6]_____ customers were lured away by cheaper prices.

Furthermore, the company has recently borrowed money from the banks,
[7]_____ increased monthly repayments and interest charges.

[8]_____ survive in this very difficult situation, we will need to reduce costs.
This may include cutting salaries and possibly reducing the number of employees.

---

2   Write a report extract of around 180 words outlining the problems your company has at the moment. Use the table below to help you. Include the following:

- Outline the problems.

- Give the reasons.

- State the result.

PROBLEM	REASON	RESULT
Sales have fallen.	Economic recession	Loss of jobs as some stores must be closed.
More competition	Customers are shopping in discount stores.	Profit loss
Unemployment figures have increased.	Technological advances have meant that there is less need for manual workers.	People have less disposable income so sales have fallen.

5 > Logistics

Vocabulary Logistics

1 Choose the correct option in italics.

> [1]*Congestion / Concern* on Britain's roads is a real problem. That's why some companies are moving away from transporting goods by road. They are dipping their toes into more innovative ways of delivering goods, like [2]*drones / suppliers* which can [3]*arrange / transport* goods more quickly than by road. They also reduce the number of [4]*packaged / damaged* goods in transit. This is good news for [5]*retailers / packers*, who often have to foot the bill to replace items.
>
> However, drones can only carry small items; large [6]*packages / distribution* still have to be transported by road.
>
> Rather than having items delivered to an address, customers can choose to have items delivered to a [7]*collection locker / courier company*, but going to get them is not only an inconvenience, but also adds to that congestion problem.

Word building – verbs, things and people

2 Complete the word tree to reveal the hidden word. Use the definitions to help you.

1 to come to a particular place in order to take something away

2 to use and control a machine or equipment

3 a way of thinking about something that seems correct and reasonable

4 the act of bringing goods, letters etc to a particular person

5 a system or method for carrying passengers or goods from one place to another

6 to start using computers and machines to do a job, rather than people

7 to supply goods to shops and companies so that they can sell them

8 to use machines to make goods or materials, usually in large numbers or amounts

9 the study of how robots are made and used

1 C						
2 O						
3 L						
4 D						
5 T						
6 A						
7 D						
8 M						
9 R						

Grammar Passive forms

1 Complete the table with the singular and plural forms of the passive.

	Present Simple passive	Past Simple passive	Future passive	Present Perfect passive
singular	is packed	1_____	2_____	has been packed
plural	3_____	were delivered	4_____	5_____
singular	is developed	6_____	7_____	8_____
plural	9_____	10_____	will be done	11_____

2 Complete the passive sentences using *just, already* or *yet*.

1 The courier loaded the packages onto the van this morning.

The packages _____ onto the van.

2 She read the email a minute ago.

The email _____.

3 The company hasn't finished the report.

The report _____.

4 Henriqué gave me the revised schedule yesterday. I don't need another copy.

I don't need another copy. I _____ the revised schedule by Henriqué.

5 Have you booked the flight to Istanbul?

Has the flight to Istanbul _____?

6 Juanita added the information you required a moment ago.

The information you require _____ by Juanita.

7 I've sent the letter to the client.

The letter _____ to the client.

3A Decide if the first sentence in each question in Exercise 5B is *active* (A) or *passive* (P).

1 ____   2 ____   3 ____   4 ____

5 ____   6 ____   7 ____

B Change the active sentences to passive and the passive sentences to active.

1 I will present the report at the next meeting.

The report _____ by me at the next meeting.

2 It has been written about by all the car reviewers.

All the car reviewers _____ about it.

3 They haven't delivered our new fridge, yet.

Our new fridge _____, yet.

4 You can do this task very easily.

This task _____ very easily.

5 The laptop is manufactured by a Japanese company.

A Japanese company _____ the laptop.

6 We won't complete the order on time.

The order _____ on time.

7 Will the project be finished by Friday?

Will you _____ the project by Friday?

Listening

1 🔊 5.01 **Listen to the beginning of this news report. What is Amazon Prime Air?**

a an Amazon event

b a drone delivery service

c Amazon's customer service department

2 🔊 5.02 **Now listen to the whole report and complete the missing letters.**

1 An e __ c __ t __ n __ event took place in Cambridge today.

2 The delivery took place in the c __ __ n __ __ y __ i __ e.

3 To receive a drone delivery you have to live close to an Amazon f __ __ f __ __ m __ __ t centre.

4 Some people believe that drone deliveries are a s __ __ e __ y r __ __ k.

5 Customers can make m__ __ t __ p __ e orders.

6 One of the items in the package was a bag of p __ p __ o __ n.

3 **Listen again and complete the flow chart with the stages (a–e) to show the process of the Amazon Prime Air delivery service.**

a drone dispatched

b goods loaded onto drone

c drone returns to fulfilment centre

d goods are selected and packaged

e Prime Air delivery service is selected

goods are ordered online

↓

1 _____

↓

order processed by Amazon

↓

2 _____

↓

goods transferred to the dispatch area

↓

3 _____

↓

customer then provides all-clear to land

↓

4 _____

↓

order delivered

↓

5 _____

Functional language

Agreeing and disagreeing

1 Complete the conversation with the correct response.

A: I think everyone should get a good bonus this year. They all hit their targets.

B: [1] *I completely agree with you. / I know they're right.*

A: However, we are still behind schedule for the latest project. We could ask all employees to work this weekend.

B: [2] *I'm not sure that's a good idea. / Good thinking.* People need to spend time with their friends and family.

A: [3] *I don't agree at all. / That might work.* Everyone wants the project to be a success. Losing one weekend won't kill them!

B: [4] *It is good yes, / That's one way of looking at it,* but they need to relax so that they have energy to come back to work on Monday. If they don't, they will all be exhausted.

A: [5] *Good thinking / That's nonsense.* Why don't we ask everyone to do an extra hour every Monday and Wednesday for the next month?

B: [6] *That's nonsense! / That would be a good solution.* I'd be happy with that.

Negotiating

2 Complete the conversation with phrases from the box.

> I'd like to hear   just to clarify   my proposal would be   how does that
> good to see   what I'd like to   are you well

A: [1]_____ you again. [2]_____ ?

B: Very well, thanks.

A: [3]_____ discuss today is the distribution centre update.

B: OK. I'm looking forward to discussing the details.

A: To start, [4]_____ from you first.

B: Sure. The first item to discuss is the new warehouse we want to buy.

A: Good. I think that has top priority at the moment.

B: [5]_____ that we increase our storage space by one fifth so that we have the capacity to expand.

A: An interesting proposal. Would this mean increasing the cost of the project?

B: Yes, but still within our budget. [6]_____ all sound to you?

A: Sounds good to me. [7]_____ , we can expand distribution by 20% without going over budget?

B: Well, between 15% and 20%.

3 Match the responses to the proposals.

1 How would you feel if we increased the number of trucks?   ____

2 We can't agree to a system update unless the staff receive more training.   ____

3 Can we look at changing the management team?   ____

4 Would you be prepared to upgrade staff salaries?   ____

a What do you mean by 'changing'?

b I'm happy to link the system update and training.

c I think we'd find an increase acceptable.

d I think that's quite reasonable for staff who take on extra duties.

Writing   Letter of complaint

1 **Complete the formal letter with missing sentences.**

a However, you did not respond to our first or subsequent emails.

b We look forward to your prompt response.

c We left messages to which you did not respond.

d You assured us that this could be arranged.

e We request that you deliver the outstanding laptops immediately.

---

44 Congress Road
Glasgow G3 8QT
31/01/2018

Re: Order #7991 50 laptops

Dear Sirs,

We ordered 50 laptops from your company on 1st February on the understanding that they would be delivered by 1st March. ¹_____
However, only 25 were delivered. We contacted you immediately by email.
²_____ We were unable to get through to your customer service department although we tried on numerous occasions. ³_____ We are very surprised by this as we are long-standing customers of yours.
I must inform you that we will be withholding payment for the computers received until we receive the rest of the order. ⁴_____
We sincerely hope that this matter can be quickly resolved to our mutual satisfaction.

⁵_____

Alain DuPont
Purchasing Manager

---

2 **Read the information in the table and write a letter of complaint to the supplier in around 180 words. Include the following:**

• Begin and end the letter appropriately.

• Use appropriate formal language.

• Use the passive where possible.

Problem	Extra details	Demand	Desired outcome
20 office chairs ordered; no chairs were delivered	Unable to get in contact with customer service department; phone calls not returned	Deliver the chairs immediately or explain why not possible	Receipt of chairs or we will place order with a different supplier

6 > Entrepreneurs

Vocabulary   **Running a business**

1 Complete the definitions with the words in the box.

| crowdfunding   business angel   go out of business |
| pitch   profit   set up   start-up   target market |

1	_____	the type of people that you aim to sell your products or services to
2	_____	to start a company or organisation
3	_____	a method of getting money for something, for example a new business venture, by asking many people to give part of the money needed, often on the internet
4	_____	money that you gain by selling things or doing business, after your costs have been paid
5	_____	a new company that has been started recently
6	_____	the things someone says to persuade people to buy something, do something or accept an idea
7	_____	stop operating
8	_____	a private investor who puts money into new business activities

2 Complete the table with the correct forms of the words.

Noun	Verb	Adjective
entrepreneur	–	1 _____
investment	2 _____	–
3 _____	finance	4 _____
5 _____	advise	advisory
fund/funding	6 _____	–
7 _____	grow	–
founder	8 _____	–

3 Complete the sentences with the correct form of the words from Exercise 2.

1 Michelle's _____ (entrepreneur) skills have made her a very successful businessperson.

2 Buying shares in Microsoft was a very sound _____ (invest).

3 The _____ (finance) world was surprised by the takeover bid.

4 Your bank can give you_____ (advise) about starting a new business.

5 The company has to get more government _____ (fund) to avoid going under.

6 The company's _____ (grow) was slow in the first quarter, but it has picked up well.

7 We need to attract a new _____ (invest) who can inject some capital into this project.

8 The company's _____ (found) has been very successful in his venture.

Grammar   Reported speech

1 **Change the sentences from direct speech to reported speech.**

1 'Have you finished preparing your presentation?' I asked Anna.

I _____ .

2 'What time do you want to break for lunch tomorrow?' Charlie asked.

Charlie _____ .

3 'Do you want to meet here on Friday?' Mary asked.

Mary _____ .

4 'How do you like your coffee?'

She _____ .

5 'I studied Economics at university.'

She _____ .

6 'Our meeting has been postponed.'

He _____ .

7 'We spoke on the phone on Tuesday.'

He _____

8 'Do you enjoy your work?'

She _____ .

2 **Change the sentences from reported speech to direct speech.**

1 He said that he was going to Paris the following week.

_____

2 Shazia asked us if we would be launching the new product soon.

_____

3 The Director told me that Violetta would be taking over from Kasper.

_____

4 He said that the new e-commerce manager would be starting work on Monday.

_____

5 Our client said that she would meet me the next day.

_____

6 Carol said that she had met the designer the day before.

_____

7 The entrepreneur said that he started his business in 2012.

_____

8 I asked the secretary if he could help me set up the room for the meeting.

_____

Listening

1 🔊 6.01 **Listen to the interview with an entrepreneur. Decide if the statements are *true* (T) or *false* (F).**

1 Linda is an engineer. ____

2 Linda's interest in Marine Biology began when she was very young. ____

3 After leaving school Linda was paid to look after turtles. ____

4 Linda decided to rid the sea of plastic after her experience on a Greek island. ____

5 They financed the project through crowdfunding. ____

6 Academics didn't believe the system would work. ____

7 Linda and Tina don't earn a lot of money. ____

8 They employ two personal assistants and a full-time accountant. ____

2 **Listen again and complete the sentences.**

1 Linda's company specialises in _____ _____ management.

2 Her partner has developed a system for cleaning up the world's _____ .

3 Linda said that she didn't have the engineering _____ to develop the system she wanted.

4 Both Linda and Tina got first-class honours _____ .

5 At first, they tried _____ institutions to raise money for their project.

6 They advertised for funds on social _____ _____ .

7 Ms Carlin is Ensign's business _____ .

8 Linda and Tina have been in this business for _____ _____ .

9 The company is making a _____ .

10 They have employed a _____ and an engineering _____ .

3 **Choose the summary that best describes Linda's venture.**

A At first Linda wasn't really interested in the sea and the creatures that live in it. She wanted to be an engineer. The sea turtles on the Greek island of Zakynthos made her want to become a marine biologist. She met Tina and together they set up a business which is now doing well. They are attempting to clean up the world's oceans.

B Linda studied marine biology at university, where she met Tina, and later she did a master's degree in business studies and marketing. This was useful when they set up their company, Ensign. The company had a few problems in the beginning as they needed to raise funds. Now the company is doing very well.

C Linda has developed a system to help protect the world's sea creatures. The innovative idea came to her when she was volunteering to help protect turtles. After doing this she went to university to study engineering. When she left university she and her business partner, Ms Carlin, set up a company that specialises in environmental clean-ups.

Functional language

Dealing with objections

1 **Complete the conversations with the words in the box.**

| ask   have   sound   deal   concerns   fair   aware   appreciate |

1 **A:** We don't think your team will complete the project by the end of the month.

B: I am _____ that time is an important factor.

2 **A:** We have already gone over budget for this year.

B: I _____ that your finances are limited.

3 **A:** It's the most expensive of all.

B: That's a _____ point, but it's the best on the market.

4 **A:** Can I _____ why this amount is a problem?

B: We need more than 10,000 to complete the order.

5 **A:** We need it as soon as possible.

B: If I can deliver in one month, do we have a _____?

6 **A:** I can take 10% off the price. How does that _____?

B: I think that will work for us.

7 **A:** We can't afford to buy it right now.

B: That doesn't _____ to be a problem.

8 **A:** What are your main _____?

B: The delivery date and the total number of units.

Presenting visual information

2 **Choose the correct option in italics.**

1 In the *next part / fact* of the presentation, I'm going to talk about our sales.

2 Now that I've finished, I will *show you / hand over* to my colleague.

3 There has been a(n) *significant / interesting* increase in sales. Up by nearly 40%.

4 When you read the contract, you need to check all the little *details / facts*.

5 I would like to *hand over / show you* a slide with our latest sales figures.

6 *You'll notice / think* that there has been a drop in the sales of women's clothing.

7 Looking more at the pie *graph / chart*, we can see that most of our budget was spent on advertising.

8 It is *significant / interesting* to see that people under 25 don't buy that brand of phone.

Writing   Summarising

1   **Read this extract from a talk made by somebody describing how their family business was started and decide which is the best title:**

a   An amazing grandmother

b   Developing a family business

c   How my grandmother started the family business

I'm the granddaughter of Silvana Medici, who sadly died before I was born. My grandmother was an amazing woman. She began her catering business way back in the 1950s as a means of earning some extra cash for her children. Her husband had died as a result of being injured in the war.

My grandmother was a cook in a wealthy household before and during the war years, but by the 1950s, there were fewer positions for her. This was because society was changing and there was little cash to employ servants. She didn't know what to do, but she knew that she had to find a way of earning a living.
I suppose she was lucky that she had a skill which she could use to her advantage: she was a very good chef.

Anyway, she started making her own cakes, jams and preserves, and selling them to local shops. They were very popular and a few local hotels began placing regular orders. She began to make desserts too, again these were bought by the local hotels.

One sunny day a man who owned a large retail business ate her produce in one of the hotels. He was very impressed with the quality of her food and made enquiries regarding the person who had made it.

He arranged to meet my grandmother and made her an offer no one could refuse – an interest-free loan. Naturally, she accepted and has never looked back. She invested the money in new kitchen equipment and employed a part-time assistant, which allowed her to produce more cakes and jams. Sales of her produce grew again and after a year she was able to open her own shop. Over the years she continued to expand the number of shops and now she has a chain of shops all over northern Italy.

---

2   **Read the first paragraph again and change it into reported speech.**

3   **Write a summary of the text in Exercise 1 in around 150 words. Include the following:**

•   Identify main topic/purpose.

•   Use synonyms and paraphrase where possible.

•   Use linking words to join sentences.

•   Use reporting verbs.

Vocabulary   Working abroad

1 Put letters in brackets in the correct order to complete the sentences.

1 It takes time for language learners to understand the _____ (uancsen) of a new language.

2 Although I know a little Spanish, I am not _____ (lueftn) in it yet.

3 Some people _____ (emoc rsacos) as disagreeable, but actually, they are nice when you get to know them.

4 People often have to travel _____ (lneoa) when they are away on business.

5 Phrase books are _____ (dlywie dseu) by tourists travelling abroad.

Adjectives, prefixes and opposites

2 Complete the table with the correct form of the words.

direct   formal   honest   kind   polite   reserved   respectful   sociable

dis-	im-	in-	un-

3 Find ten words with the prefixes *un-*, *dis-* and *im-* in the wordsearch.

D	I	S	R	E	S	P	E	C	T	F	U	L	L	H
I	R	A	D	F	E	R	T	Y	U	K	N	P	O	P
S	D	F	A	B	D	E	Y	N	M	L	R	O	U	O
H	G	G	H	I	E	R	T	M	I	O	E	R	U	L
O	H	H	I	N	F	O	R	M	A	L	S	D	N	K
N	U	I	S	H	E	R	L	O	B	N	E	E	H	U
E	U	N	S	O	C	I	A	B	L	E	R	S	E	N
S	S	O	I	F	K	I	E	T	R	S	V	D	L	T
T	B	V	N	S	J	D	J	P	U	E	E	A	P	V
A	E	I	D	A	F	H	Y	S	N	V	D	C	F	E
S	F	G	I	S	A	C	V	H	K	I	U	S	U	A
D	J	O	R	G	U	N	F	R	I	E	N	D	L	Y
U	N	F	E	S	G	N	P	O	N	S	R	N	U	Z
G	E	W	C	C	H	K	I	L	D	R	I	Y	N	O
J	I	M	T	T	I	M	P	O	L	I	T	E	A	G

Grammar   Past tenses: Past Simple, Past Continuous and Past Perfect Simple

1 Complete the table with the correct form of the verbs.

Past Simple	Past Continuous	Past Perfect
I discovered	I [1]_____	I [2]_____
you [3]_____	you were travelling	you [4]_____
we [5]_____	we [6]_____	we had forgotten
he lived	he [7]_____	he [8]_____

2 Choose the correct option in italics.

1 Last week we *held / were holding* the meeting in the main auditorium.

2 When Amir *taught / had taught* in Japan he suffered from culture shock at first.

3 The best thing about working abroad is that I *learned / had been learning* about different cultures.

4 Heidi *studied / was studying* in London when I first met her.

5 Consuela was excited because she *didn't travel / hadn't travelled* to that part of the world before.

6 Rukshana *was already living / lived* in the UAE when she moved to the Dubai office.

7 Gabriella *worked / had worked* in many countries after joining the firm.

3 Choose the correct option to complete the exchanges.

1 Have you finished preparing your presentation yet?

a I finished it before I went home yesterday.

b I had finished it last night.

c I was finishing it last night.

2 Where were you going when I saw you earlier?

a I went to the stationary office to sign out more paper.

b I was going to lunch in the canteen.

c I had been to the marketing department.

3 When had the law firm closed?

a It was closing for six years now.

b It closed a month ago when the partners retired.

c It had closed two months before the building was bought.

4 When did you go to New York?

a I didn't go in the end. I went to Boston instead.

b I was going to San Francisco instead.

c I had gone last year.

Reading 1 **Read the text and put the paragraphs into the correct order.**

Culture Shock 🖎

A _____

Finally, one of my friends from home came for a visit. She dragged me out of the house, insisting that I showed her around the city. In the beginning that was a nightmare, but her enthusiasm started to rub off on me and I began to enjoy exploring again.

B _____

Culture shock can quickly become a very real problem when you're working abroad. It happens to different people at different times. Some people feel totally alienated from their new surroundings almost as soon as they step out of the plane. Others are so excited to be in a foreign country that they don't think about the emotional effect of the cultural differences they encounter until the novelty of being in a new country wears off.

C _____

Shortly after that, I began to feel strange and didn't want to go anywhere. I had to go out of course, as I needed to buy food and go to work. However, I found that I was shutting myself off from my colleagues and was put off by socialising. I stayed in my apartment and didn't leave it for several weeks, except to go to work and buy food on my way home.

D _____

When she left, I was afraid that I would lapse back into my 'culture shock shell' but, by that time, I had made friends with some of my colleagues, so I had people to explore with outside work hours. At one stage I almost gave up and went back home. I'm very glad now that I didn't. I never looked back and really enjoy living and working in my host country.

E _____

I tend to be one of those people who soak up the atmosphere. I am very curious and want to know everything immediately. When I first arrived in my host country, I tried hard to integrate into the culture by stopping locals in the street and practising my new language skills, but I was met with a frosty reception. It didn't occur to me that I had asked too many questions – that I had annoyed people. Later, in my new apartment, I realised that the problem had to do with cultural differences.

2 **Read the text again and complete the sentences with a word from the text.**

1 Culture shock often makes newcomers feel _____ from their new environment.

2 When some people first _____ an unfamiliar culture, they are taken in by the excitement.

3 She had not thought that she would _____ people with all her questions.

4 She detached herself from her _____ and became isolated.

5 Her friend's _____ for sightseeing brought her out of her shell.

6 She began to _____ places again.

7 Now she is happy that she did not leave her _____ country.

3 **What is the tone of this text?**

a negative

b positive

c balanced

Functional language

Expressing preferences

1 **Complete the sentences with the words in the box.**

| would were prefer is mind keen |

1 The new manager is very _____ on the idea. He really likes it!

2 The construction company _____ rather wait another month before starting the project.

3 The CEO doesn't _____ helping after she's finished her work.

4 If it _____ up to the staff, we would move to a more central location.

5 We'd _____ not to launch the product before summer.

6 Their preference _____ to expand in Shanghai.

2 **Complete the sentences with the correct form of the verb.**

1 I'm keen *to finalise / finalising* the objectives.

2 I don't mind *delay / delaying* the meeting till this afternoon.

3 If it *is / were* up to me, I'd recruit some more people for the next stage.

4 We're happy *let / to let* central office make the final decision.

5 I'd rather not *relying / rely on* the new system till it's been tested.

6 I'm not keen on *making / to make* a decision without your agreement.

7 We'd prefer *to communicate / communicating* with the overseas offices directly.

8 They just want *to make / making* sure that there are no problems later on.

Keeping a conversation going

3 **Match the answers (a–h) with the questions (1–8).**

1 Where did you go on holiday?

2 What are you working on at the moment?

3 What do you do?

4 What sort of programmes do you make?

5 I understand you play a lot of badminton. Is that right?

6 What do you think of the new office?

7 I've just come back from a trip to Rome. Have you ever been to Italy?

8 You know, I also studied archaeology, like you.

a I make documentaries. I'm working on one at the moment about the financial crisis.

b Really? How did we both end up working in an office?

c I don't know. I haven't seen it yet.

d I went to Australia.

e I'm a teacher during the day and I play the drums in a band at the weekend.

f Yes, that's right. I play every weekend.

g I'm working on a new ad campaign with the Paris team.

h No, but I'm thinking about going for a long weekend. Would you recommend it?

Writing Making recommendations

1 Quickly read the extract from a report outlining cross-cultural issues within a company and decide if the language used is:

a formal

b informal

c neutral

2 Complete the report with the words in the box.

suggest advise essential obvious would

Report on cross-cultural issues within the company

It has become ¹_____ that there are issues in the workflow of our Dublin–Dubai project. These have apparently been caused by cross-cultural differences between the colleagues working on the project in the two offices. The project is very important to our company and if it fails, no doubt our profits will be adversely affected in the next quarter. It is therefore ²_____ that the cross-cultural teams begin to work together by understanding how their cultures differ.

We ³_____ you to try to engage the staff together in an activity away from the project which they are collaborating on. We hope that this will ease tensions between the parties and also allow them to learn about and appreciate their different cultural approaches.

Our recommendation ⁴_____ be to organise a day of team-building activities through an external company. This would take the teams off site and engage them in a sporting or leisure activity in which they all have to work together towards a common goal. We ⁵_____ that this is organised without delay to avoid any further misunderstandings.

3 Look at the notes below. Write a report of about 180 words. Include the following:

- Give suggestions, advice and make recommendations.

- Offer advice and make one other suggestion.

- Use the functional language from the report in Exercise 2 in the coursebook where appropriate.

Issue of cross-cultural disagreements

Staff unable to agree on workflow methods – projects delayed

Recommendation

Suggest / Advise
- pair staff from different cultures to work together
- arrange cross-cultural training
- appoint a member of staff with a cross-cultural background to oversee the project

8 ➤ Leadership

Vocabulary   Leadership

1 Use the clues to complete the crossword.

Across

2 a duty to be in charge of something, so that you make decisions and can be blamed if something bad happens

5 to get something you want because of your efforts or abilities

6 a piece of work that must be done, especially one that is difficult or that must be done regularly

Down

1 to give part of your work to someone in a lower position than you

3 to put several things in order of importance, so that you can deal with the most important ones first

4 a group of people who have been chosen to work together to do a particular job

2 Choose the correct word in italics.

1 If staff don't *prioritise / trust* their manager, they won't work well.

2 Ashley's promotion means she will have more *priority / responsibility* and important decisions to make.

3 Building a *task / team* can be very difficult at first.

4 Making key *responsibilities / decisions* is not always easy.

5 We should *set / win* goals and aim at increasing our profit margins by 20%.

6 It's important to *give / make* clear instructions so everyone knows exactly what to do.

7 Let's make sure that our work is of a very high *priorities / standard*.

8 When you give feedback, it should be *constant / constructive*.

3 Put the words in the correct order to complete the sentences.

1 manager / a / tasks / good / when / delegate / to / knows

_____

2 your department / running / have / a / as / cope with / to / manager / you

_____

3 decisions / must / able / a / key / manager / be / make / to

_____

4 a / respect / manager / important / to / new / for / it's / gain

_____

5 set / work / and / them / towards / you / to / need / goals

_____

6 effort / if / we / we / can / complete / make / time / on / an / the project

_____

Grammar Relative clauses

1 **Match 1–7 with a–g to complete the sentences.**

1 These days, businesses need flexible leaders

2 This is the report

3 There's a new course on leadership

4 Delhi is

5 During the week,

6 Jamil is the one

7 The conference,

a which was on Monday, was very interesting.

b that you requested.

c where the call centre is located.

d whose paper was well received at the conference.

e which I would like to attend.

f who are innovative and can implement new ideas.

g when everyone is going to work, the roads are congested.

2 **Choose the correct word in italics. Decide if the clauses in the sentences are *defining* (D) or *non-defining* (ND).**

1 It's Barcelona *where / when* the conference is being held.   ____

2 Ms Romain, *who / that* is our guest speaker, is very famous.   ____

3 It's today *where / when* we will find out who is going to be promoted.   ____

4 Jack, *whose / that* video we saw, is our marketing manager.   ____

5 That's the file *that / where* I was looking for yesterday.   ____

6 I think we first met in March 2016 *where / when* we were at
   the neuroscience conference.   ____

7 Wasn't it Pierre, *who / whose* father is a famous neurosurgeon,
   that first introduced us?   ____

3 **Complete the sentences using the words in the box. Use some words more than once.**

when   where   which   who   whose

1 Everyone _____ was at the meeting agreed that we should adopt a new sales strategy.

2 Manuel, _____ idea it was to split the department into two, has now been made manager.

3 I think it was in August, _____ it was really hot, that we had problems with the air-conditioning system.

4 This is the person _____ car was stolen from the company car park.

5 *The Financial Times*, _____ is my favourite newspaper, is no longer being delivered.

6 Do you recall the time _____ we worked without modern technology?

7 Isn't that the woman _____ gave the keynote speech ?

8 Wasn't it in Karachi, _____ our head office is, that the seminar was held?

Listening

1 🔊 8.01 **Listen to the first part of a business training session about three types of leadership and choose the correct answers.**

Type 1 – Authoritarian

1 Authoritarian leaders think that a
- **a** flat structure works best.
- **b** hierarchical structure works best.

2 Their main priority is the
- **a** performance of the company.
- **b** morale of their employees.

3 This type of leader
- **a** avoids difficult decisions.
- **b** makes difficult decisions quickly.

4 They are best suited to
- **a** creative projects.
- **b** areas which do not involve working directly with people.

5 The danger with this type of leader is
- **a** employees may become demotivated.
- **b** not achieving short-term goals.

Type 2 – Democratic

1 This type of leader
- **a** likes talking with their team members.
- **b** prefers to limit communication with their employees.

2 Regarding decision making,
- **a** they pass it on to their team.
- **b** they do it all themselves.

3 Their strong point is to
- **a** understand situations from other people's point of view.
- **b** make other people see their point of view.

4 Companies value this type of leader
- **a** more than type 1.
- **b** less than type 1.

5 Their main priority is to
- **a** meet deadlines and targets.
- **b** create high-quality products.

Type 3 - Delegative

1 Delegative leaders
- **a** let their team make decisions.
- **b** make decisions in consultation with the team.

2 They are good at
- **a** providing support for their team.
- **b** asking their team if they need support.

3 Delegative leaders
- **a** provide their team with the necessary resources.
- **b** let their team provide their own resources.

4 This type of leader works best with
- **a** relatively inexperienced people.
- **b** older, more motivated people.

5 The delegative style
- **a** can cause some staff to lose direction.
- **b** helps increase motivation.

2 🔊 8.02 **Listen to the second part of the training session. Match the type of leader to the speakers.**

Speaker 1   Authoritarian

Speaker 2   Democratic

Speaker 3   Delegative

Functional language

Giving and responding to feedback

1 Complete the conversation with words from the box.

> good that you   I don't think   your responsibility   in future if
> really impressed with   very good job   could have asked   saying is that

1 What Maria is _____ you need to deal with the problem as soon as it appears.

2 I think _____ you give yourself more time, that might make it easier to keep to the deadline.

3 You _____ any one of us for help, that would have resulted in a quicker solution.

4 He was trying to do too many things at the same time, but _____ he realised that.

5 The manager is _____ the work he did. She thought it was excellent.

6 It was _____ arranged a meeting with the CEO. It was the right thing to do.

7 It was _____ to check all the paperwork on the takeover, but you left it to someone with less experience.

8 You did a _____ of delegating the work on that project. Well done!

Leading and managing meetings

2A Match 1-8 with a-h to complete the sentences.

1 I can understand what you're saying is important,

2 Let's meet again on Wednesday

3 The goal for this meeting

4 Is everyone OK

5 This has been a very

6 OK, let's begin by thinking

7 The new advertising campaign

8 Please send me your report

a is to decide who will go to the Milan office.

b productive meeting.

c but please let John finish.

d by close of business on Tuesday.

e to finalise everything.

f isn't on today's agenda.

g about the latest drop in sales figures.

h with their tasks?

B Match the complete sentences in 2A (1-8) with their functions (a-e).

a Opening the meeting

b Managing interruptions

c Reviewing the discussion

d Referring to action points

e Next steps

Writing   Informing of a decision

1   **Read the email and put the letters in brackets in the correct order.**

To: Santiago Sanchez

From: All managers

Subject: Meeting decision

Dear Colleagues,

This is to ¹_____ (mifron) you of our decisions arrived at in yesterday's meeting about our future international structure and its leadership.

There we reached a ²_____ (nssceouns) regarding the establishment of a new international division. This will closely supervise the operations in our foreign locations. Senior management will report to myself, the CEO, to begin with. We will monitor the international division closely at first, but we hope that, in time, the senior managers will gain autonomy.

Secondly, we ³_____ (drgeea) to appoint Adnan al-Haroun as Senior Manager of this new division. He will be responsible for overseeing operations in our international markets. When these expand, we will open subsidiary offices in the foreign locations to which we export.

The final decision made at the meeting was to confirm the appointment of our new Export Manager, Daniela Marquez. She will replace Henry Smythe, who, as you ⁴_____ (wnko), is retiring next month.

We will ⁵_____ (nnouanec) these decisions at a press conference on Friday.

I would like to take this opportunity to congratulate you all on our success.

Kind regards,
Santiago

2   **Look at the meeting notes below and write a formal email of about 180 words to inform staff of the decisions made. Include the following:**

- All the points in the notes.
- Formal language.
- The functional language from Exercise 2 in the coursebook.

Point discussed	Decision
Export manager under pressure	Open more overseas offices, to be staffed by managers from headquarters initially, then recruit local managers.
Language barrier for senior managers working in local markets	Senior managers to attend language courses; training to start next month urgently
Current National Sales Manager leaving next month	Appoint new manager.

Pronunciation

Unit 1

1.1 Word stress

1 Match the words (a–o) with the stress patterns (1–5).

1 Oo   _____   _____   _____

2 Ooo   _____   _____   _____

3 oO   _____   _____   _____

4 oOo   _____   _____   _____

5 oOoo   _____   _____   _____

a audit	**f** event	**k** payroll
b financial	**g** promotion	**l** supply
c environment	**h** glamorous	**m** priorities
d ensure	**i** invoicing	**n** recruitment
e finance	**j** immediate	**o** quality

2 🔊 P.1.1 Listen and check. Then listen again and practise saying the words.

3 Write the stress pattern for these words.

1 employee   _____

2 image   _____

3 imagine   _____

4 interesting   _____

5 manages   _____

6 manufacturing   _____

7 organisation   _____

8 responsibilities   _____

9 satisfaction   _____

10 supervisor   _____

4 🔊 P.1.2 Listen and check. Then listen again and practise saying the words.

1.3 Intonation and politeness

5 🔊 P.1.3 Listen to these questions and mark the main stressed word.

1 Which countries have you worked in?

2 Did you have a good journey?

3 Are you going to the conference?

4 How's business at the moment?

5 Which hotel are you staying in?

6 What are your plans for tomorrow?

7 What time do you have to leave?

8 Have you got any questions?

9 Is there anything I can help you with?

10 Will you be at the meeting next week?

6 Listen again. Practise saying the questions with the same stress and intonation as in the recording.

Unit 2

2.1 Stress in compound nouns

1 Choose the phrase which has a different stress pattern from the others.

	a		**b**		**c**	
1	**a** bank account		**b** customer loyalty		**c** plane ticket
2	**a** client management		**b** email account		**c** loyalty card
3	**a** brand loyalty		**b** business card		**c** hotel booking
4	**a** advertising brochure		**b** customer satisfaction		**c** marketing campaign
5	**a** credit card		**b** customer services		**c** luxury industry
6	**a** booking system		**b** business plan		**c** key customer
7	**a** bank statement		**b** business model		**c** online shopping
8	**a** debit card		**b** jewellery company		**c** mobile broadband

2 🔊 P.2.1 Listen and check.

3 Practise saying the phrases with the correct stress pattern.

2.2 Connectors: intonation and pausing

4 🔊 P.2.2 Listen and practise saying the connectors.

1 Originally, …

2 Traditionally, …

3 In recent times, …

4 Now, …

5 Nowadays, …

6 In the future, …

7 Twenty years ago, …

8 Twenty years from now, …

5 🔊 P.2.3 Listen and mark where the speaker pauses.

1 Originally, the global luxury industry moved only from west to east.

2 Traditionally, long-established brands were the most popular.

3 In recent times, there have been global changes.

4 Now, more and more Asian brands are appearing in American shops.

5 Nowadays, France is the top destination for wealthy Chinese shoppers.

6 In the future, Asian brands may be as popular as Western ones.

7 Twenty years ago, nobody would have expected these developments.

8 Twenty years from now, the situation may have changed beyond recognition.

6 🔊 P.2.3 Listen again and practise saying the sentences.

Unit 3

3.1 Stress in derived words

1 Complete the sentences with the correct form of the words in brackets. Underline the stressed syllable in the word you have added.

1 _____ (commit) is a so-called soft skill.

2 Job-seekers face a lot of _____ (compete).

3 What does the _____ (express) 'come across well' mean?

4 We're looking for a Key Account _____ (manage).

5 How would you describe your _____ (personal)?

6 Would you apply for a job if you didn't have the necessary _____ (qualify)?

7 Willingness to travel is a key _____ (require).

8 Have you ever applied for an _____ (intern)?

9 I've written five job _____ (apply) this week.

10 Her résumé is _____ (impress).

2 ◀ P.3.1 Listen and check.

3 Practise saying the sentences in Exercise 1.

3.2 Voice range and intonation in indirect questions

4 ◀ P.3.2 Listen and underline the word with the main stress.

1 Can you tell me something about your previous experience?

2 I'd like to know whether you'd be prepared to work overtime.

3 Could you tell me what your greatest passion is?

4 I'd be interested to know something about your computer skills.

5 Can you give me some more details about your previous job?

6 Could you say if you'd be willing to do some training?

7 I'd like to know when you'd be able to start.

8 Could you explain why you decided to leave your previous job?

5 Practise saying the questions in Exercise 4.

Unit 4

4.3 /iː/, /ɪ/, /eɪ/ and /aɪ/

1 Write the words.

1 /fiːl/	_____	**11** /griːn/	_____
2 /eɪt/	_____	**12** /ˈlɪmɪt/	_____
3 /traɪ/	_____	**13** /diːl/	_____
4 /dɪˈleɪ/	_____	**14** /reɪz/	_____
5 /rʌɪt/	_____	**15** /stɪl/	_____
6 /liːd/	_____	**16** /staɪl/	_____
7 /leɪt/	_____	**17** /waɪt/	_____
8 /lɪst/	_____	**18** /dɪˈsaɪd/	_____
9 /weɪt/	_____	**19** /streɪt/	_____
10 /fɪl/	_____	**20** /striːt/	_____

2 ◀ P.4.1 Listen and check.

3 Practise saying the words.

4.4 Intonation in 'OK'

4 ◀ P.4.2 Listen to the different ways of saying 'OK' and match them with their uses.

Speaker 1   ____

Speaker 2   ____

Speaker 3   ____

Speaker 4   ____

A Getting people's attention.

B Asking someone to agree with you.

C Showing that you understand and agree.

D Showing that you understand what someone says but you don't necessarily agree.

5 ◀ P.4.3 Listen and use arrows to mark the rising (up) or falling (down) intonation of 'OK'.

1 OK, can I have everyone's attention, please?

2 I think it's time for a break. OK?

3 OK, let's get down to business.

4 Let's meet at two o'clock, OK?

6 Listen again and practise saying the sentences, using the same intonation and pausing as in the recording.

Unit 5

5.1 Pausing and stress in presentations

1 P.5.1 **Listen to part of a presentation and mark the places where the speaker pauses.**

With the orders packed, they are ready to leave the warehouse and begin the next stage in the process – delivery to the customer. Delivery can be undertaken by the postal service or by courier companies. Frequently, customers are able to track the progress of their package online.

Consumers enjoy the convenience of having goods delivered to their homes. Of course, customers are not always at home to receive their package.

One solution is to use these: they are called collection lockers. Packages can be left inside and the customer can pick them up at any time by entering a PIN number.

The logistics that e-commerce relies upon are developing all the time. In the future, we may see some changes in the way our online shopping is delivered.

This robot has been designed to deliver packages. Customers can arrange to collect their goods from the robot via a mobile app. Some companies are also considering using drones to transport goods to customers.

2 **Listen again and practise saying the presentation.**

5.2 Auxiliary verbs in passives

3 P.5.2 **Listen to these sentences and underline where the speaker uses contractions.**

1 Logistics can be defined as the business of transporting things to the place where they are needed.
2 The advertisement has been viewed 85 million times.
3 A self-driving lorry has already been designed.
4 Drivers will be given new tasks.
5 The driver will be able to get out of the truck and rest while it's unloaded and loaded.
6 Drivers are not going to be made completely redundant.
7 This robot has been designed to deliver packages.
8 When the orders have been packed, they are delivered to the customer.

4 P.5.3 **Listen to the sentences and underline where the speaker uses weak forms.**

1 The advertisement with the splits stunt was made to demonstrate the effectiveness of the steering system.
2 Self-driving systems for lorries and buses have been developed.
3 Drivers aren't going to be made completely redundant.
4 This robot's been designed to deliver packages.
5 Experiments are being conducted with drones.
6 When the orders have been packed, they are delivered to the customer.
7 Goods can be collected from the robot via a mobile app.
8 Logistics can be defined as the business of transporting things to the place where they're needed.

5 **Practise saying the sentences in Exercise 4. Pay attention to the weak forms and contractions.**

Unit 6

6.1 Consonant–vowel linking

1 🔊 P.6.1 **Listen to these phrases and mark the consonant–vowel links between the words.**

1 at the top of the building

2 linked in to the system

3 it lasts a week or two

4 this is the fourth attempt

5 do you feel OK?

6 more than seven hours later

7 set off an alarm

8 watch all the programmes

2 **Listen again and practise saying the phrases.**

3 🔊 P.6.2 **Listen and mark the consonant–vowel links in these sentences.**

1 Under what circumstances would you start a business?

2 What would be the right kind of business for you?

3 What are the three biggest attractions and disadvantages of running your own business?

4 The amount of business done over period of time is called turnover.

5 Demand is the need or desire that people have for particular goods and services.

6 What are some of the difficulties of the fast growth of a start-up like Fairphone?

7 A business angel is someone who gives a business money, often in exchange for a share of the company.

8 What types of consumers might be interested in buying your products or services?

9 The company reduces its impact on the environment by recycling minerals.

10 Which of the business ideas would you invest in?

4 **Listen again and practise saying the sentences.**

6.4 Intonation and discourse marking in presentations

5 🔊 P.6.3 **Listen to these presentation extracts. Mark where the speaker pauses.**

1 This morning I'd like to give you a quick update on the progress we've made so far.

2 If you look at this bar chart, you can see how the markets compare.

3 These figures give a clear indication of how sales have grown.

4 On this slide you can see a summary of what I've told you so far.

5 Next, let's move on to customer age demographics.

6 What's especially interesting in this chart is the left-hand column.

7 I'd like to finish by showing you a forecast for the next six months.

8 If you have any questions, I'll be very happy to answer them.

6 **Listen again and practise saying the sentences, using the same intonation and pausing as in the recording.**

Unit 7

7.2 Phrasing and intonation in past sentences

1 ◀ P.7.1 **Listen and mark the two main stresses in each sentence.**

1 Things were going well in 2007, which is when Pawel moved to the States.

2 But he'd only been there a year when the economic crisis happened.

3 It was the first time he'd lived abroad, and he immediately noticed lots of small differences.

4 When he was talking to people, he realised that communication was much faster.

5 While he was walking to the office, he saw sidewalks that suddenly ended in the middle of nowhere.

6 He'd never seen anything like that before, so he was pretty surprised.

7 He hadn't worked for a global corporation before, and he found the style of communication rather different.

8 Because he hadn't been to the States before, he wasn't used to distances being measured in minutes.

2 **Listen again. Practise saying the sentences with the same stress and intonation as in the recording.**

7.3 Strong or weak?

3 ◀ P.7.2 **Listen to these sentence chunks and underline the main stressed words. The number of stressed words is given in brackets.**

1 as for me (2)

2 I think the process is important (2)

3 but not as important as the result (2)

4 if the group can't reach a decision (2)

5 the person responsible has to make one (1)

6 deadlines can be moved around (2)

7 but only if they really have to be (2)

8 I think once decisions have been made (2)

9 you should respect them (1)

10 even if you don't agree with them (2)

4 **Before you listen, decide if the words in italics will be in their *strong form* (S) or *weak form* (W).**

1 *As __ for __ me*, I think *the __* process *is __* important, yes, but not *as __* important *as __ the __* result.

2 If *the __* group can't reach *a __* decision, *the __* person responsible *has __ to __* make one.

3 Deadlines *can __* be moved around, but only if they really *have __ to __* be.

4 I think once decisions *have __ been __* made, you should respect *them __* , even if you don't agree with *them __* .

5 It's good *to __* reach *a __* consensus if *you __ can __* , but it isn't always possible.

6 If *you __* want *to __* be perceived *as __* competent, *you __* should respect deadlines.

7 Decisiveness is even more important *than __* consensus.

8 *You __* should act *as __ a __* group, even if *there __ are __* disagreements in *the __* group.

5 ◀ P.7.3 **Listen and check. Then listen again and practise saying the sentences.**

Unit 8

8.1 Glottal stops

1 🔊 P.8.1 **Listen and write whether the letter 't' is pronounced as /t/ (t) or as a glottal stop (g).**

1 I can't understand. ____

2 I've got to go. ____

3 I've got an idea. ____

4 What are you wearing? ____

5 There's a lot going on. ____

6 Sit on the floor. ____

7 Wait for me. ____

8 Let me help. ____

2 🔊 P.8.2 **Listen and underline where you hear a glottal stop instead of a /t/ sound.**

1 Just got a taste of what it's like to be in charge.

2 To what extent is it entertainment and to what extent is it educational?

3 A good manager knows when to delegate jobs.

4 The new manager is finding it hard to win his staff's respect.

5 Making tough decisions is an essential part of leadership.

6 Staff aren't going to trust you if you don't care about what they think.

7 I'm not sure you're right this time.

8 In what ways can a manager set an example for the team?

8.2 Phrasing and intonation in relative clauses

3 🔊 P.8.3 **Listen and add commas to the sentences which contain non-defining relative clauses.**

1 The meeting which was scheduled to start at 10 o'clock was delayed by half an hour.

2 The room where the meeting was due to be held hadn't been cleaned or prepared.

3 We need staff who can adapt to changing circumstances.

4 My friend and colleague who works in the next office is away on a training course.

5 One of the managers who has worked here for over 30 years is retiring next month.

6 Is it possible for people who have a fixed mindset to change how they think?

7 Abbie Smith who works at Chicago Booth Business School has looked at the benefits for companies that appoint 'frugal' executives.

8 Entrepreneurs who are less afraid of risks than managers are better at taking 'hot' decisions.

9 What are the five key elements which are required to develop neuroleadership skills?

10 A new book which has the title *Neuroscience for Leadership* points out the need for years of practice, reflection and feedback.

4 **Listen again and practise saying the sentences. Remember to pause after the comma.**

Answer key

Unit 1

Vocabulary
1 1 heads 2 take care 3 running
4 report
5 responsible 6 journalist
7 actor

2 1 b 2 c 3 c 4 a 5 b 6 b

3 1 Bureaucracy 2 hierarchy
3 promotion 4 innovative
5 decentralised 6 centralise

Grammar
1 1 f, g 2 b, d 3 a, c 4 e, h

2 1 I won't be in the office on
Tuesday.
2 Are you going to the meeting
later?
3 We're visiting the conference
centre next week.
4 I think Lamar is going to get a
promotion soon.
5 We don't have to leave early on
Monday.
6 Our flight won't leave on time
in this weather.
7 Faiza will chair the meeting on
Thursday.
8 The conference isn't going to
finish until late.

3 1 is going – plan/arrangement
2 's going to drive – personal
intention
3 have – plan/arrangement
4 is going to be – prediction
5 starts – a scheduled event
6 Are you going to come –
personal intention
7 have – plan/arrangement

Reading
1 1 F – ... Médecins Sans Frontières
(MSF), or Doctors without
Borders, was founded in 1971.
2 T – In the beginning, there
were only thirteen doctors and
journalists. ... including the
thirteen original founders.
3 F – The following year (1975),
MSF assisted in its first refugee
crisis, ...
4 T – During the 70s, there were
problems for the MSF staff on
the ground; there was little
preparation before staff set off
on a mission; doctors had little
support and supply lines were
not reliable.
5 F – The organisation employs ...
and include logisticians, heads
of fundraising, coordinators,
managers and accountants.
6 F – He or she [the manager]
must also ensure that projects
don't go over budget.
7 F – The coordinator develops
and implements training
programmes ...

2 1 b – By 1972 there were 300
volunteers, including the
thirteen original founders. In
that year, MSF's first task ...
2 b – The following year MSF
assisted in its first refugee crisis,
helping Cambodians who had
fled their country.
3 d – ... there were no
humanitarian logisticians ...
4 b – The manager and
coordinator train volunteers to
do their jobs.
5 d – The coordinator develops
and implements training
programmes ...
6 b – The coordinator develops
and implements training
programmes and is responsible
for making travel arrangements
and arranging meetings.

3 a

Functional language
1 1 d 2 c 3 f 4 a
5 g 6 e 7 b

2 1 Can I take your coat
2 Can I get you something to
drink
3 Is it your first time in the Mexico
office
4 When did you join the company
5 Where are you based
6 Do you work with Beena
7 Do you report to Charu Patel
8 Are you free for dinner this
evening

Writing
1 1 Madam
2 inform
3 Further
4 After
5 hesitate
6 questions
7 sincerely

2 1 D 2 B 3 A 4 E 5 C

3 **Model answer**
Good morning Amalia,
Thank you for your email
regarding the Digital Marketing
conference.
There are six people attending, so
you are all going by train. My PA is
booking the tickets this afternoon
and they can be collected from the
ticket office at the central station.
As there are six people from this
company going, most of the
workshops can be attended. I
would like you to attend those
which outline new marketing
strategies, please.
I look forward to receiving your
report on your return.
Regards,
Eleni

Unit 2

Vocabulary
1 1 image 2 base 3 growth
4 engagement
5 approach 6 history
7 venture 8 loyal

2 1 brand stretching
2 core business 3 devalue
4 product placement
5 loyalty
6 ultra-luxury
7 interactive marketing

3 1 product placement
2 brand stretching
3 interactive marketing
4 core business
5 devalue
6 loyalty
7 ultra-luxury

Grammar
1 1 First of all – For instance
is usually followed by an
example.
2 but – contrasts what has
happened with what is
happening now; and adds
information.
3 For example – it is followed by
an example; However contrasts
information.
4 and – adds information; but
contrasts it.
5 Although – contrasts
information; In addition adds to
information given already.
6 as well as – adds ideas; to start
with begins a sequence of ideas.
7 In addition – adds information;
for instance is followed by an
example.
8 However – contrasts
information and ideas; also
adds information and ideas.

2 1 b – but contrasts ideas.
2 g – when contrasts information.
3 h – as well as adds information.
4 d – while contrasts ideas.
5 e – although contrasts
information.
6 c – and sequences ideas.
7 a – however contrasts
information.
8 f – in addition adds information.

3 1 a – contrasting information
2 a – contrasting information
3 b – also adds information;
although introduces contrasting
information.
4 b – then sequences information;
for instance introduces an
example.
5 b – First of all sequences
information; For instance
introduces an example.

6 b – *Although* contrasts information; *Recently* refers to time.

7 a – *but* contrasts information; *for example* introduces an example.

8 b – *In addition* adds information; *Such as* introduces an example, but cheaper products are not an example of the Bulgari range.

Listening

1 **1** F – *It's not often that I am invited to give a talk on the radio, so I am delighted to be here.*

2 F – *Having said that, the business has expanded ... to include tops made from cotton, merino wool, cashmere and silk ...*

3 T – *I began to knit and design jumpers for myself when I was about thirteen.*

4 T – *I sold them in local boutiques ...*

5 F – *I needed to learn business skills, so I enrolled on a course.*

6 T – *... She wore my tops in her TV series and so I had product placement ... It's great publicity!*

7 T – *I was tempted to stop hand-knitting the jumpers, but realised that this wasn't a good idea as they would no longer be unique.*

8 F – *... I hope to retire somewhere nice and cool where I can wear my woolly jumpers.*

2 **1** b – *The name is misleading now: the brand has grown to include tops made from cotton, merino wool, cashmere and silk.*

2 a – *I couldn't believe that my tops were so popular.*

3 b – *The jumpers sold themselves because each one is original.*

4 c – *I was selling the garments in the States and the UK.*

5 d – *Many clients have since written to say that they never buy any other tops but mine ... it was then I realised that brand loyalty is really very important.*

6 d – *We're looking into a software package that will take care of it.*

7 c – *I'm planning to retire in a few years' time so that's something to concentrate on.*

3 c

Functional language

1 **1** tried **2** afraid **3** important **4** would **5** should **6** able

2 **1** talk **2** to take **3** working **4** to give **5** do **6** to reschedule **7** to spend

3 **1** c **2** e **3** b **4** d **5** f **6** a

Writing

1 **1** delighted **2** held **3** invited **4** collaboration **5** confirm **6** forward **7** regards

2 **1** Thank you **2** the invitation **3** I'm afraid **4** be unable **5** I hope **6** best regards

3 **Model answer**
Dear Mr Schmidt,
Thank you very much for the invitation to the opening ceremony for your new conference facilities. My partner and I would be delighted to accept your invitation.
We very much look forward to seeing you.
Kind regards,
Victor Kreuz

Unit 3

Vocabulary

1 **1** employers **2** jobseekers **3** stand out from **4** be of value to **5** come across well **6** clichéd

2 **1** internship **2** employer **3** competition **4** jobseekers **5** communication **6** motivation

3 **1** recruiter **2** flexible **3** character **4** position **5** internship **6** skill

F	H	F	**C**	F	K	M	V	A	X
M	J	S	**H**	J	H	P	**F**	D	E
S	O	A	**A**	D	U	O	**L**	F	T
E	P	C	**R**	E	**P**	F	**E**	G	Y
R	L	B	**A**	B	**O**	V	**X**	K	R
T	K	U	**C**	N	**S**	**K**	**I**	**L**	**L**
K	E	I	**T**	M	**I**	L	**B**	L	N
L	E	M	**E**	V	**T**	C	**L**	S	A
R	**E**	**C**	**R**	**U**	**I**	**T**	**E**	**R**	Y
O	T	W	K	E	**O**	D	Z	O	L
I	**N**	**T**	**E**	**R**	**N**	**S**	**H**	**I**	**P**

Grammar

1A **1** D **2** I **3** D **4** I **5** D **6** D **7** I **8** I

B **1** I'd like to know if you are prepared to move if you get this job.

2 What did you like most about your last job?

3 Can you tell me why you applied for this job?

4 Have you worked abroad?

5 Could you tell me how you found out about this job?

6 I'd like to know why you left your last job.

7 Who do you admire most in your present company?

8 What do you think your main weakness is?

2 **1** Could you tell me a little more about yourself?

2 I'd like to know how many years you worked for your last employer.

3 Please tell me why you left your previous job.

4 I'd like to know more about your responsibilities in your last job.

5 I need to ask if you would consider applying for an internship.

6 I wonder if you could say more about your ambitions.

7 Could you tell me if you would emigrate for the job?

8 I'd like you to tell me about your leadership experience.

Reading

1 **1** E – *It can be quite scary ... there are several useful tips that jobseekers can follow.*

2 A – *mould your experience to fit the job description ... Play up the skills you have that are needed for the job.*

3 C – *Find out as much as you can about the company you are applying to.*

4 D – *Think about the questions you could ask in your interview.*

5 F – *Don't lie.*

6 B – *the more you can demonstrate how eager you are ...*

2 **1** a **2** b **3** c **4** a **5** b **6** a **7** c

Functional language

1 Clarifying / Exploring — 3, 5
Summarising / Paraphrasing — 1, 10
Checking understanding — 7, 9
Correcting — 4, 8
Giving feedback — 2, 6

2 **1** e **2** b **3** d **4** a **5** f **6** c

3 **1** Thank you for your time today.

2 Could you tell me more about the training programme?

3 I haven't had that exact experience.

4 Can I speak to some of the people I would be working with?

5 I look forward to hearing from you

6 That's a good question.

Writing

1 **1** vacancy **2** advertised **3** enclosed **4** degree **5** confident **6** experience **7** asset **8** grateful

2 Model answer

Dear Ms Arshad,

I am writing to apply for the position of Marketing Manager advertised on your website. I hold a master's degree in International Marketing. I have been working as a Marketing Manager for the last three years, as you can see from my CV. I run a very successful international marketing team and divide my time between leading my team at the main office and travelling to our key markets. I feel that I have all the qualities you require in a successful candidate.

I have very innovative ideas to offer and a good track record of putting them into practice. I am a confident public speaker and provide excellent presentations. I now feel the need to face new challenges and responsibilities. I believe that the job you have advertised would suit my skills and abilities.

I would very much appreciate the opportunity to meet with you and learn more about the role. I look forward to hearing from you in the near future.

Thank you for taking the time to read my letter.

Yours sincerely,

Unit 4
Vocabulary
1 1 takeover 2 opportunities 3 product 4 strategies 5 major

2 1 b 2 b 3 d 4 a 5 a

3 1 expand 2 profitable 3 development 4 acquire 5 succeed 6 growth 7 merger 8 risky 9 failure

Grammar
1 1 should – It is a good idea to do this.
2 must – It is necessary to do this.
3 don't have to - It isn't necessary to do this.
4 mustn't – This is not allowed/permitted.
5 should – It is a good idea to do this.
6 must – It is necessary to do this.
7 mustn't – This is not allowed/permitted.
8 don't have to –It isn't necessary to do this.

2 1 have to – *will* isn't used with modal verbs. It is necessary to do this.
2 don't have to – *should* is used for something that is a good idea. It isn't necessary to do this.

3 shouldn't – It's not a good idea to do this.
4 mustn't – This is not allowed/permitted.
5 should – It's a good idea
6 have to – *will* isn't used with modal verbs. It is necessary to do this.
7 should – It is a good idea to do this.
8 mustn't – This is not allowed/permitted.

3 1 don't have to – It isn't necessary to do this.
2 must – It is necessary to do this.
3 have to – It is necessary to do this; *will* isn't used with *must* or *should*.
4 shouldn't – It isn't necessary to do this.
5 have to – This has the same meaning as *must*; *will* isn't used with modal verbs.
6 must – It is necessary to do this.
7 should – It's a good idea to do this.
8 mustn't – It isn't allowed/permitted to do this.

Reading
1 1 D – The first sentence says these are not strategy; 'either' refers back to the first example of what is not strategy.
2 F – After saying what is not strategy, this sentence gives a definition of it. The following sentence repeats 'unique value'.
3 A – *This opening sentence continues to define what value is.*
4 E – *But* contrasts with the fact that the company is small and yet *its operating margin of over 15% is exceptionally high among Japanese manufacturers.*
5 C – A continuation of the previous paragraph: it is successful. Also, the topic of babies is linked to the following sentence.
6 B – Topic sentence which introduces a new theme. The following sentence then echoes the word *market*.

2 1 T – *... the term is somewhat mysterious*
2 F – It should aim to *provide unique value.*
3 F – *But managers' biggest responsibility is to draw up a blueprint for building a distinct corporate identity.*
4 F – *But its operating margin of over 15% is exceptionally high among Japanese manufacturers.*
5 T – *... Pigeon's sales have risen by about 50% over the past five*

years, *thanks to rapid growth overseas.*
6 T – *'We owe our success to many failures in the past.'*

3 c

Functional language
1 1 A anything, B fine
2 A hand, B Could
3 A Would, B offering
4 A Let, B appreciate
5 A like, B mind

2 1 exactly
2 How about
3 pick up
4 building on
5 doable
6 sense
7 not sure
8 take this on

Writing
1 1 Due 2 has led 3 so 4 have resulted in 5 As a result 6 because 7 resulting in 8 In order to

2 Model answer

Report on Current Problems

Our supermarket chain has faced considerable problems this year. This report aims to outline the main ones.

Main Problems and Reasons

Our sales figures have fallen considerably. Our current poor financial outlook is mainly due to the national economic recession. New government policies and taxes are making it difficult for businesses. Therefore, there will have to be some store closures and, as a consequence, the loss of a number of jobs.

Moreover, we are now faced with more competition from discount stores which are offering consumers prices which we cannot compete with. This has led to a loss of revenue. However, it is our belief that these customers will return once the novelty of discounted food has worn off.

The third factor in the downturn is that unemployment levels have increased recently. Technical advances have meant that there is less need for manual labour. As a result, people have less money to spend at our stores. This, in turn, has had an adverse effect on our sales figures.

Unit 5
Vocabulary
1 1 Congestion 2 drones 3 transport 4 damaged 5 retailers 6 packages

7 collection locker

2 **1** collect **2** operate **3** logic
4 delivery **5** transport
6 automate **7** distribute
8 manufacture **9** robotics
Hidden word: logistics

Grammar

1 **1** was packed **2** will be packed
3 are delivered
4 will be delivered
5 have been delivered
6 was developed
7 will be developed
8 has been developed
9 are done **10** were done
11 have been done

2 **1** have already been loaded
2 has just been read
3 hasn't been finished yet
4 have already been given
5 been booked yet
6 has just been added
7 has already been sent

3A **1** A **2** P **3** A **4** A **5** P
6 A **7** P

B **1** will be presented
2 have written **3** hasn't been
delivered **4** can be done
5 manufactures
6 won't be completed **7** finish

Listening

1 b

2 **1** exciting **2** countryside
3 fulfilment **4** safety risk
5 multiple **6** popcorn

3 **1** e **2** d **3** b **4** a **5** c

Functional language

1 **1** I completely agree with you.
2 I'm not sure that's a good idea.
3 I don't agree at all.
4 That's one way of looking at it.
5 Good thinking.
6 That would be a good solution.

2 **1** Good to see
2 Are you well
3 What I'd like to
4 I'd like to hear
5 My proposal would be
6 How does that
7 Just to clarify

3 **1** c **2** b **3** a **4** d

Writing

1 **1** d **2** a **3** c **4** e **5** b

2 **Model answer**
Re: order #6957 20 office chairs
Dear Sirs,
We ordered twenty office chairs
from your company on 6th June
on the understanding that they
would be delivered by 20th June.
You assured us that this would
be arranged and we would have
delivery on time.
However, they still have not been
received. We have contacted

you by email, but have not had a
response yet. Also, we have been
unable to make contact with your
customer service department by
phone. We have left messages to
which we have yet to receive a
response.
As we are long-standing
customers of yours, we are very
surprised at this lack of response.
We are now requesting that the
chairs be delivered immediately or
receive an explanation as to why
this is not possible.
I must inform you that if you
do not respond to this letter
immediately, we will be forced to
cancel the order and an order will
be placed with another supplier.
However, we sincerely hope that
this situation can be resolved.
We look forward to your prompt
response.
Purchasing manager

Unit 6

Vocabulary

1 **1** target market **2** set up
3 crowdfunding **4** profit
5 start-up **6** pitch
7 go out of business **8** business
angel

2 **1** entrepreneurial **2** invest
3 finance **4** financial **5** advice/
advisor **6** fund **7** growth
8 found

3 **1** entrepreneurial **2** investment
3 financial **4** advice **5** funding
6 growth **7** investor **8** founder

Grammar

1 **1** asked Anna if/whether she
had finished preparing her
presentation – We often use *ask
if/whether*, then change the
verb tense. Here the Present
Perfect changes to the Past
Perfect.
2 asked (me) what time I wanted
to break for lunch the next/
following day – *me*, the object,
can be added in indirect speech,
however, it is not always
necessary; *tomorrow* changes
to the *next/following day*; *want*
in the present tense changes to
the Simple Past.
3 asked (me) if/whether I wanted
to meet there on Friday – *if/
whether* is used in reported
questions; *here* becomes *there*
in reported speech; the verb,
want, changes from the Present
Simple to the Past Simple.
4 asked (me) how I like/liked my
coffee – You could use either
like as it remains true or *liked*
(Past Simple) for reported
speech depending on the
situation.

5 said that she had studied
Economics at university –
change the Past Simple to Past
Perfect.
6 said that our/their meeting had
been postponed – we use *our*
or *their* depending on who's
meeting it was; Present Perfect
Simple tense becomes Past
Perfect Simple.
7 said that we/they had spoken
on the phone on Tuesday – we
often change the person to the
pronoun and the adverbs of
time and place when we change
from direct speech to reported
speech; Past Simple changes to
Past Perfect.
8 asked (me) if/whether I enjoyed/
enjoy my work – we use *ask if/
whether* to report questions;
we can use either *enjoy* as
it remains true or *enjoyed*
because the verb changes from
Present Simple to Past Simple;
you and *your* becomes *I* and *my*.

2 **1** 'I'm going to Paris next week,'
he said. – *He* becomes *I* and
the *following* becomes *next* in
direct speech. The Past Simple
tense changes to the Present
Simple in direct speech.
2 'Will you be launching the new
product soon?' asked Shazia. –
Would becomes *will* in direct
speech.
3 'Violetta will be taking over
from Kasper,' the Director said.
– the Past Simple becomes the
Present Simple.
4 'The new e-commerce manager
will be starting work on
Monday,' he said. – Future tense
would changes to *will.*
5 'I'll meet you tomorrow,' our
client said. – *The next day*
becomes *tomorrow* and *I*
replaces *she*, *me* changes to
you. *Would* becomes *will* in
direct speech.
6 'I met the designer yesterday,'
Carol said. – *Carol* changes to *I*
and *the day before* changes to
yesterday in direct speech.
7 'I started my business in
2012,' the entrepreneur said. –
The *entrepreneur* becomes *I* and
as the statement is still true, the
tense doesn't change.
8 'Can you help me set up the
room for the meeting?' I
asked (the secretary). – *If* is
unnecessary in direct speech,
and *could* becomes *can*.

Listening

1 **1** F – *Linda is the CEO of Ensign.*
2 T – *I've always been fascinated
by the sea and marine life
and school biology lessons
reinforced that, so I decided*

that I wanted to become a marine biologist.

3 F – *I took a year off to volunteer on a Greek island protecting loggerhead turtles.*

4 T – *So was it this experience that made you want to clean up the water? – Yes, that's right.*

5 T – *Tina had been reading about crowdfunding and suggested we try it.*

6 T – *... we tried academic institutions, but they just weren't interested ... they said that our idea wouldn't work.*

7 F – *We are making a profit and enough money to pay ourselves good salaries.*

8 F – *... we have a PA and an engineering assistant for Tina. We outsource other tasks. We don't employ someone to do our accounts, for example.*

2 1 marine waste 2 seas
3 knowledge 4 degrees
5 academic 6 media sites
7 angel 8 two years 9 profit
10 PA, assistant

3 B

A is incorrect because Linda had always been interested in the sea and the creatures that live in it and she didn't say that she wanted to be an engineer.

C is incorrect because Tina, not Linda, designed and built the system. The idea came to Linda while she was on a Greek island protecting loggerhead turtles. She didn't study engineering. Ms. Carlin is Linda's business angel. The company specialises in waste management.

Functional language

1 1 aware 2 appreciate
3 understand 4 ask 5 say
6 sound 7 have 8 concerns

2 1 next part 2 hand over
3 a significant 4 details
5 show you 6 notice 7 chart
8 interesting

Writing

1 c

2 The speaker said that she was the granddaughter of Silvana Medici, who had sadly died before she was born. She said that her grandmother had been an amazing woman who had begun her catering business way back in the 1950s as a means of earning some extra cash for her children. Her husband had been injured in the war and had died.

3 **Model answer**
The speaker's grandmother began a catering business in the 1950s, because she needed money for her children as her husband had died

of an injury sustained in the war. Before the war, she had worked as a cook in people's houses, but after the war, there were fewer jobs for servants.
She needed to earn money and needed a job to support her children. She decided to use her culinary skills and began her business by making popular cakes, preserves, and later desserts. Local shops and hotels started to make regular orders, then soon enough a retailer offered her a job. She accepted and never looked back.

Unit 7
Vocabulary

1 1 nuances 2 fluent
3 come across 4 alone
5 widely used

2 *dis-* dishonest, disrespectful
im- impolite
in- indirect, informal
un- unkind, unreserved, unsociable

3

```
D I S R E S P E C T F U L L H
I R A D F E R T Y U K N P O P
S D F A B D E Y N M L R O U O
H G G H I E R T M I O E R U L
O H H I N F O R M A L S D N K
N U I S H E R L O B N E E H U
E U N S O C I A B L E R S E N
S S O I F K I E T R S V D L T
T B V N S J D J P U E E A P V
A E I D A F H Y S N V D C F E
S F G I S A C V H K I U S U A
D J O R G U N F R I E N D L Y
U N F E S G N P O N S R N U Z
G E W C C H K I L D R I Y N O
J I M T T I M P O L I T E A G
```

Grammar

1 1 was discovering
2 had discovered 3 travelled
4 had travelled 5 forgot
6 were forgetting 7 was living
8 had lived

2 1 held – Past Simple for a completed action in the past
2 taught – Past Simple for a completed action in the past
3 learned – Past Simple for a completed action in the past
4 was studying – Past Continuous for an action that was in progress in the past when it was interrupted by another action
5 hadn't travelled – Past Perfect for an action that happened before a past event
6 was already living – Past Continuous for a continuous action in the past interrupted by another action
7 worked – Past Simple for a completed action in the past

3 1 a – Past Simple for completed action in the past
2 b – tense agreement: Past

Continuous for an action that was in progress in the past
3 c – tense agreement: Past Perfect for an action completed before another action in the past
4 a – tense agreement: Past Simple for an action completed in the past

Reading

1 A 4 B 1 C 3 D 5 E 2

2 1 alienated 2 encounter
3 annoy 4 colleagues
5 enthusiasm 6 explore
7 host

3 c

Functional language

1 1 keen 2 would 3 mind
4 were 5 prefer 6 is

2 1 to finalise 2 delaying 3 were
4 to let 5 rely 6 making
7 to communicate 8 to make

3 1 d 2 g 3 e 4 a 5 f
6 c 7 h 8 b

Writing

1 a

2 1 obvious 2 essential 3 advise
4 would 5 suggest

3 **Model answer**
Recently it has become obvious that there are cross-cultural differences in some of our overseas teams, causing misunderstandings and affecting workflow and deadlines. In some of our offices we have colleagues working from several different cultures. They generally only visit the overseas offices for a short period so there isn't enough time for them to become fully familiar with each other's methods of working, which are often influenced by their cultural background.
We advise that you try to pair members of staff together from different cultures to work closely on projects together. This will enable them to get to know their colleagues and understand their cultural differences. We would also recommend that your arrange cross-cultural training as soon as possible. This can be resourced outside the company and there are many training providers which specialise in this.
It is essential that everyone tries to work together to overcome this issue and for that reason we recommend you put these steps into effect immediately. If these

recommendations do not have the desired effect, we suggest that you appoint a member of staff with a cross-cultural background to oversee any projects affected. He or she can then implement a suitable cross-cultural workflow.

Unit 8

Vocabulary

1 1 delegate 2 responsibility
3 prioritise 4 team 5 win
6 task

2 1 trust (trust a person, prioritise things)

2 responsibility (be responsible for, make decisions and delegate)
3 team (build a team, do a task)
4 decisions (key decisions – collocation)
5 set (set goals – collocation)
6 give (give instructions – collocation)
7 standard (collocation – high standard)
8 constructive (constructive feedback – collocation)

3 1 A good manager knows when to delegate tasks.
2 As a manager you have to cope with running your department.
3 A manager must be able to make key decisions.
4 It's important for a new manager to gain respect.
5 You need to set goals and work towards them.
6 If we make an effort, we can complete the project on time.

Grammar

1 1 f 2 b 3 e 4 c 5 g 6 d
7 a
2 1 where – D
2 who – ND
3 when – D
4 whose – ND
5 that – D
6 when – D
7 whose – ND
3 1 who 2 whose 3 when
4 whose 5 which 6 when
7 who 8 where

Listening

1 **Type 1:** 1 b 2 a 3 b 4 b 5 a
Type 2: 1 a 2 a 3 a 4 b 5 b
Type 3: 1 a 2 a 3 a 4 b 5 a
2 **Speaker 1:** Democratic
Speaker 2: Delegative
Speaker 3: Authoritarian

Functional language

1 1 saying is that
2 in future if
3 could have asked
4 I don't think
5 really impressed with
6 good that you
7 your responsibility
8 very good job

2A 1 c 2 e 3 a 4 h 5 b 6 g
7 f 8 d

B 1 b 2 e 3 a 4 d 5 c 6 a
7 b 8 e

Writing

1 1 inform 2 consensus
3 agreed 4 know 5 announce

2 **Model answer**
From: Juan Blunt CEO
To: All managers
Subject: Board meeting decision
This is to inform you of the decisions made at yesterday's board meeting about our export department and its future.
First of all, we agreed to open more overseas offices in the countries we export to. This should take the pressure off our Export Manager. We made this decision because of our rapid growth in this area. The offices will initially be staffed by managers in our headquarters until we can recruit local managers who are familiar with the various locations. Secondly, we finally reached a consensus regarding the training programmes we need to implement. We have decided that all senior managers should be given language courses as needed in the languages they will be liaising in. We would ideally like to appoint native speakers of the languages, but for the moment we are limited in what we can do. As this is a matter of urgency, training will start next month.
Our final decision was to appoint Consuela Martinez as National Sales Manager to take over from Mr Branch who is leaving the company next month.

Pronunciation

Unit 1

1 A audit, finance, payroll
B glamorous, invoicing, quality
C ensure, event, supply
D financial, promotion, recruitment
E environment, immediate, priorities

3 1 ooO 2 Oo 3 oOo 4 Ooo
5 Ooo 6 ooOoo 7 oooOo
8 oooOoo 9 oooo 10 Oooo

5 1 Which countries have you worked in?
2 Did you have a good journey?
3 Are you going to the conference?
4 How's business at the moment?
5 Which hotel are you staying in?
6 What are your plans for tomorrow?
7 What time do you have to leave?
8 Have you got any questions?
9 Is there anything I can help you with?
10 Will you be at the meeting next week?

Unit 2

1 1 b 2 a 3 c 4 b 5 b 6 c
7 c 8 c

5 1 Originally, | the global luxury industry moved only from west to east.
2 Traditionally, | long-established brands were the most popular.
3 In recent times, | there have been global changes.
4 Now, | more and more Asian brands are appearing in American shops.
5 Nowadays, | France is the top destination for wealthy Chinese shoppers.
6 In the future, | Asian brands may be as popular as Western ones.
7 Twenty years ago, | nobody would have expected these developments.
8 Twenty years from now, | the situation may have changed beyond recognition.

Unit 3

1 1 Commitment 2 competition
3 expression 4 Manager
5 personality 6 qualifications
7 requirement 8 internship
9 applications 10 impressive

4 1 Can you tell me something about your previous experience?
2 I'd like to know whether you'd be prepared to work overtime.
3 Could you tell me what your greatest passion is?
4 I'd be interested to know something about your computer skills.
5 Can you give me some more details about your previous job?
6 Could you say if you'd be willing to do some training?
7 I'd like to know when you'd be able to start.
8 Could you explain why you decided to leave your previous job?

Unit 4

1 1 feel **2** eight/ate **3** try
4 delay **5** right/write **6** lead
7 late **8** list **9** wait **10** fill
11 green **12** limit **13** deal
14 raise **15** still **16** style
17 white **18** decide
19 straight **20** street

4 **Speaker 1** C
Speaker 2 A
Speaker 3 D
Speaker 4 B

5 1 OK↓
2 OK↑
3 OK↓
4 OK↑

Unit 5

1 With the orders packed, / they are ready to leave the warehouse / and begin the next stage in the process / – delivery to the customer. / Delivery can be undertaken by the postal service / or by courier companies. / Frequently, / customers are able to track the progress of their package online. / Consumers enjoy the convenience of having goods delivered to their homes. / Of course, / customers are not always at home to receive their package. / One solution is to use these: / they are called collection lockers. / Packages can be left inside / and the customer can pick them up at any time / by entering a PIN number. / The logistics that e-commerce relies upon / are developing all the time. / In the future, / we may see some changes in the way our online shopping is delivered. This robot / has been designed to deliver packages. / Customers can arrange to collect their goods from the robot / via a mobile app. / Some companies / are also considering using drones to transport goods to customers.

3 1 Logistics can be defined as the business of transporting things to the place where they're needed.
2 The advertisement's been viewed 85 million times.
3 A self-driving lorry's already been designed.
4 Drivers'll be given new tasks.
5 The driver'll be able to get out of the truck and rest while it's unloaded and loaded.
6 Drivers aren't going to be made completely redundant.
7 This robot's been designed to deliver packages.

8 When the orders have been packed, they're delivered to the customer.

4 1 The advertisement with the splits stunt was made to demonstrate the effectiveness of the steering system.
2 Self-driving systems for lorries and buses have been developed.
3 Drivers aren't going to be made completely redundant.
4 This robot's been designed to deliver packages.
5 Experiments are being conducted with drones.
6 When the orders have been packed, they're delivered to the customer.
7 Goods can be collected from the robot via a mobile app.
8 Logistics can be defined as the business of transporting things to the place where they're needed.

Unit 6

1 1 at the top_of the building
2 linked_in to the system
3 it lasts_a week_or two
4 this is the fourth_attempt
5 do you feel_OK?
6 more than seven_hours later
7 set_off_an_alarm
8 watch_all the programmes

3 1 Under what circumstances would you start_a business?
2 What would be the right kind_ of business for you?
3 What_are the three biggest_ attractions and_disadvantages_ of running your_own business?
4 The amount_of business done_ over_a period_of time_is called turnover.
5 Demand_is the need_or desire that people have for particular goods_and services.
6 What_are some_of the difficulties_of the fast growth_ of_a start-up like Fairphone?
7 A business angel_is someone who gives_a business money, often_in_exchange for_a share of the company.
8 What types_of consumers might be interested_in buying your products_or services?
9 The company reduces_its impact_on the environment by recycling minerals.
10 Which_of the business_ideas would you invest_in?

5 1 This morning | I'd like to give you a quick update on the progress we've made so far.
2 If you look at this bar chart, | you can see how the markets compare.

3 These figures | give a clear indication of how sales have grown.
4 On this slide | you can see a summary of what I've told you so far.
5 Next, | let's move on to customer age demographics.
6 What's especially interesting in this chart | is the left-hand column.
7 I'd like to finish | by showing you a forecast for the next six months.
8 If you have any questions, | I'll be very happy to answer them.

Unit 7

1 1 Things were going well in 2007, which is when Pawel moved to the States.
2 But he'd only been there a year when the economic crisis happened.
3 It was the first time he'd lived abroad, and he immediately noticed lots of small differences.
4 When he was talking to people, he realised that communication was much faster.
5 While he was walking to the office, he saw sidewalks that suddenly ended in the middle of nowhere.
6 He'd never seen anything like that before, so he was pretty surprised.
7 He hadn't worked for a global corporation before, and he found the style of communication rather different.
8 Because he hadn't been to the States before, he wasn't used to distances being measured in minutes.

3 1 As for me
2 I think the process is important
3 but not as important as the result
4 if the group can't reach a decision
5 the person responsible has to make one
6 deadlines can be moved around
7 but only if they really have to be
8 I think once decisions have been made
9 you should respect them
10 even if you don't agree with them

4 1 As S for W me, I think the W process is S important, yes, but not as W important as W the W result.
2 If the W group can't reach a W decision, the W person responsible has S to W make one.

3 Deadlines *can* S be moved around, but only if they really *have* S *to* W be.

4 I think once decisions *have* W *been* W made, you should respect *them* W, even if you don't agree with *them* W.

5 It's good *to* W reach *a* W consensus if *you* W *can* S, but it isn't always possible.

6 If *you* W want *to* W be perceived *as* W competent, *you* W should respect deadlines.

7 Decisiveness is even more important *than* W consensus.

8 *You* W should act *as* W *a* W group, even if *there* W *are* W disagreements in *the* W group.

8 Entrepreneurs, who are less afraid of risks than managers, are better at taking 'hot' decisions.

9 What are the five key elements which are required to develop neuroleadership skills?

10 A new book, which has the title *Neuroscience for Leadership*, points out the need for years of practice, reflection and feedback.

Unit 8

1
1 t
2 glottal stop
3 t
4 glottal stop
5 glottal stop
6 t
7 glottal stop
8 glottal stop

2
1 Just got a taste of what it's like to be in charge.
2 To what extent is it entertainment and to what extent is it educational?
3 A good manager knows when to delegate jobs.
4 The new manager is finding it hard to win his staff's respect.
5 Making tough decisions is an essential part of leadership.
6 Staff aren't going to trust you if you don't care about what they think.
7 I'm not sure you're right this time.
8 In what ways can a manager set an example for the team?

3
1 The meeting, which was scheduled to start at 10 o'clock, was delayed by half an hour.
2 The room where the meeting was due to be held hadn't been cleaned or prepared.
3 We need staff who can adapt to changing circumstances.
4 My friend and colleague, who works in the next office, is away on a training course.
5 One of the managers, who has worked here for over 30 years, is retiring next month.
6 Is it possible for people who have a fixed mindset to change it how they think?
7 Abbie Smith, who works at Chicago Booth business school, has looked at the benefits for companies that appoint 'frugal' executives.

Audioscripts

🔊 2.01

It's not often that I am invited to give a talk on the radio, so I am delighted to be here. So, I've been asked to talk about how I started my business and how my knitwear became the well-known, top-selling brand, Woolly. The logo is, of course, a sheep. Having said that, the business has expanded since it was named and the brand has grown to include tops made from cotton, merino wool, cashmere and silk, so they're for all seasons, not just winter.

I began to knit and design sweaters (jumpers) for myself, when I was about thirteen. I used to buy cheap balls of wool in the sales, and then made them into colourful jumpers. They were all original, and still are today. Friends wanted to buy them, so when I left school I went into the business of producing jumpers which were all original and handmade. I sold them in local boutiques and soon I had a good client base. I couldn't believe that my tops were so popular. The jumpers sold themselves because each one is original. I had to employ other people to help knit them and soon there were twenty working for me and we were selling them all over the country.

I decided that if my business was to expand further, I needed to learn business skills, so I enrolled on a course. After that I became more confident and decided to approach a well-known actress to become the face of my brand. She wore my tops in her TV series and so I had product placement, just like that. It's great publicity! Sales increased dramatically and I had to take on more staff. I was tempted to stop hand-knitting the jumpers, but realised that this wasn't a good idea as they would no longer be unique. People wanted one-off original handmade sweaters and that's what I gave them. Of course, this made the garments very expensive, but there was certainly a demand for them. Luxury items are always costly.

I was selling the garments in the States and the UK, but soon I was getting queries and requests for specific designs from customers in France, Germany, the Netherlands and Denmark. Here we had real customer engagement, which is not something I had considered before. Many clients have since written to say that they never buy any other tops but mine. That was very encouraging, and it was then I realised that brand loyalty is really very important. What surprised me was that clients would be happy to order tops well in advance, so that their orders would be ready as the season arrived.

At the moment, I'm trying to venture into Asian markets. I am taking a cautious approach because I need to have my catalogues translated into languages such as Urdu, Hindi, Thai, Mandarin and Japanese. We're looking into a software package that will take care of it. I have to find reliable translators and interpreters for my marketing team, too. It would be easier to employ local people, really, but how do I source them?

I'm planning to retire in a few years' time so that's something to concentrate on. I have loyal staff who can run the business for me, and I hope to retire somewhere nice and cool where I can wear my woolly jumpers and knit just for fun!

🔊 5.01

Good morning. I'm reporting from Cambridge in the UK, where an exciting event is taking place. Amazon UK is attempting its first drone customer delivery. The first ever delivery is low-key. The only person around is the customer themselves.

🔊 5.02

Good morning. I'm reporting from Cambridge in the UK, where an exciting event is taking place. Amazon UK is attempting its first drone customer delivery. The first ever delivery is low-key. The only person around is the customer themselves. The drone delivery is happening in the countryside. The package has just been dropped off carefully and the drone has taken off again.

Let's think for a moment about how the drone got here. The customer ordered their goods online and selected Prime Air delivery service. If you live within 7 miles – or 11 kilometres – of an Amazon fulfilment centre and your order doesn't weigh too much, you may be eligible to have goods delivered to your front garden by drone.

The order was then processed by Amazon. The goods were then selected at the centre, packaged and transferred to the dispatch section where they are taken on by the drone. The customer provides the all-clear to land to Amazon.

The drone is then dispatched. Currently drones must fly under a height of 122 metres. That means that unless a drone was flying over an airport when a plane was taking off or landing, there wouldn't be threat of collision. That's reassuring, as there have been concerns about what impacts drones will have on air traffic control if they fly close to airports.

The drone completes its delivery within the prescribed thirty-minute window, depositing the customer's order outside the home of the customer. The order is now complete, and the drone goes back to the fulfilment centre (or distribution centre to you and me).

In 2016, Amazon sold an incredible 600 items a second. Think about how many drones would've been needed to ship items. Multiple orders can be made by customers, of course, and as long as the weight limit is not exceeded, they can be dispatched via a single drone. Some might say that could cause a safety risk.

Well, the first drone to deliver a package to an Amazon customer carried a bag of popcorn and an Amazon Fire TV stick. Customers who subscribe to Amazon Prime Air can choose from numerous items to be delivered by drone, all part of the service. Of course, a drone can only carry packages that weigh up to 2.6 kilograms so you couldn't buy a desk and have it delivered by drone, at least for the moment. Who knows what the future might bring!

🔊 6.01

I = Interviewer **L** = Linda

I: I'd like to welcome Linda Gass to our programme today. You may have heard of her; she is one of our up-and-coming young entrepreneurs. Linda is the CEO of Ensign, a young company specialising in marine waste management. Her partner, Tina, who is an engineer, is the brains behind a new clean-up system for the world's seas. Welcome to the programme, Linda.

L: Thank you!

I: To begin with, Linda, perhaps you can tell us how this all started.

L: Sure, I'd be delighted to. I've always been fascinated by the sea and marine life and school biology lessons reinforced that, so I decided that I wanted to become a marine biologist.

I: And so you did!

L: Yes, but I took a year off to volunteer on a Greek island, protecting loggerhead turtles.

I: So was it this experience that made you want to clean up the water?

L: Yes, that's right. Tourism and fishing pollution create huge problems for marine life.

I: But you didn't do anything immediately?

L: No. I didn't have the knowledge that was needed to build a system that could rid the sea of plastic. Luckily, when I was in university, I met Tina and she had the engineering knowledge that I lacked. We hit it off as soon as we met and became great friends. We encouraged each other to do our practical projects for our courses. We both got first-class honours degrees and then moved in together to do our master's degrees.

I: And you did yours in Business Studies and Marketing, I believe.

L: That's right. That's helped a lot, especially when we needed funding to build the system that Tina designed.

I: And how did you raise the money?

L: Well, to begin with, we tried academic institutions, but they just weren't interested. So, Tina had been reading about crowdfunding and suggested we try it. In the beginning, I said that it wasn't a good idea. I wanted our work to be recognised by professors and other academics. I knew that we could help the world's seas and oceans, but they said that our idea wouldn't work.

I: And they were wrong!

L: Yes. We advertised for funds on social media sites and persuaded reputable journalists to write about our work. We set up Ensign and haven't looked back. We have a wonderful business angel, Ms Carlin, who has ploughed funds into our work and found us new backers, so now we're going from strength to strength with several new projects in the pipeline.

I: And how long have you been in this business?

L: Only two years in fact, although it seems more like ten because of all the experience we've had. I can't believe how lucky we've been. We're making a profit and enough money to pay ourselves good salaries.

I: Are you the only employees in Ensign?

L: Well, we were to start with, when we set up, but now we have a PA and an engineering assistant for Tina. We outsource other tasks. We don't employ someone to do our accounts, for example.

I: And you find that works?

L: So far but, of course, I think that soon we will need one on a full-time basis.

I: How about the marketing? Do you do that alone?

L: No. Tina and I both have a hand in that and so does Ms Carlin. She's full of innovative ideas.

I: Well, it was very interesting talking to you Linda and I look forward to hearing about your next project.

L: Thank you.

🔊 8.01

In today's training session, we're going to look at three different types of leader – how they work, their strengths and weaknesses, and the areas or business in which they are most successful.

The first type of leader, commonly known as the authoritarian, or autocratic, leader, believes in a hierarchical structure where decisions are passed down from senior management to the rest of the staff. They are performance-focused, that is they put the company's performance before other considerations such as staff morale or career development. They don't regard other people's feelings as important and do not show emotion. They tend to distance themselves from their staff and are usually seen only when giving presentations or on important social occasions. In some companies this kind of leader may be valued for being cool under pressure and able to make tough decisions and make them quickly. They are also valued for achieving targets and being highly profitable. This type of leadership tends to work best in areas such as production which involves manual or automated labour where there is less face-to-face contact. In more extreme cases, this type of leader may have a very low level of empathy and make decisions that damage the morale of the company and lead to long-term dissatisfaction even though short-term aims are achieved.

Next, we have the democratic leader. They enjoy open communication and sharing responsibility. They also enjoy risk-taking and thinking of new and perhaps radical solutions. They give their staff freedom to work in a way that best suits them but at the same time they will take responsibility and make the final decision. They are happy to mentor less experienced team members and believe that training and long-term career development is important. They have a high level of empathy and do show their emotions. When a project is successful, they are happy to share the credit with their team and recognise and reward the performance of talented team members. They are not as focused on profit-orientated performance as autocratic leaders and may not be as highly valued by a company because they may not meet their targets and deadlines as reliably. However, the quality of what they produce tends to be higher than that produced under autocratic leadership. They are generally more successful in flat company structures working in creative areas such as product development and design.

At the other end of the scale, there are the leaders who delegate responsibility and pass on decision making to their team members, the delegative leader. They provide helpful guidance to team members if they request it and they will make sure that the team has all the resources that they need to do the job. This kind of leadership tends to work best when the team members are highly skilled, highly motivated and mature enough to take responsibility for their actions, for example technicians in a research laboratory. It tends to work less well when team members are less experienced and need the support of someone more experienced. In these cases, a delegative style may lead to poor motivation and lack of direction.

🔊 8.02

OK. Let's move on to the next part of this session. I would like you to imagine this situation at work. The manager of a medium-sized department in a large company receives a memo from headquarters saying their office has to downsize and reduce staff numbers from 30 to 25, which means firing five people. Now, thinking about the description of the three types of leader we looked at in the first session, what would each type of leader do? Let's listen and find out.

Speaker 1
I would ask everyone to attend a meeting and explain the situation. I'd ask everyone to express their opinion and to suggest some creative solutions. I would ask them whether they would consider the idea of job sharing - two people doing one job. I think an open and direct discussion should be encouraged and would take their ideas on board. I would weigh up the pros and cons after the meeting and then let them know my decision.

Speaker 2
I would send an email to everyone explaining the situation. I would ask the team to organise a meeting to discuss what they want to do and then let me know. I would then pass their request on to the Human Resources department. If Human Resources did not accept the team's suggestion, I would ask the team to meet again and come up with another proposal.

Speaker 3
I would check the performance records of the whole team and choose the five people I think are underperformers. I would pass the list on to the Human Resources department and ask them to send the five people a letter saying that their employment will be terminated at the end of the legally required period of one month.

1.1 Word stress

🔊 P.1.1

1 audit, finance, payroll
2 glamorous, invoicing, quality
3 ensure, event, supply
4 financial, promotion, recruitment
5 environment, immediate, priorities

🔊 P.1.2

employee image imagine
interesting manages manufacturing
organisation responsibilities
satisfaction supervisor

1.3 Intonation and politeness

🔊 P.1.3

1 Which countries have you worked in?
2 Did you have a good journey?
3 Are you going to the conference?
4 How's business at the moment?
5 Which hotel are you staying in?
6 What are your plans for tomorrow?
7 What time do you have to leave?
8 Have you got any questions?
9 Is there anything I can help you with?
10 Will you be at the meeting next week?

2.1 Stress in compound nouns

🔊 P.2.1

1 bank account, customer loyalty, plane ticket
2 client management, email account, loyalty card
3 brand loyalty, business card, hotel booking
4 advertising brochure, customer satisfaction, marketing campaign
5 credit card, customer services, luxury industry
6 booking system, business plan, key customer
7 bank statement, business model, online shopping
8 debit card, jewellery company, mobile broadband

2.2 Connectors: intonation and pausing

🔊 P.2.2

1 Originally, ...
2 Traditionally, ...
3 In recent times, ...
4 Now, ...
5 Nowadays, ...
6 In the future, ...
7 Twenty years ago, ...
8 Twenty years from now, ...

🔊 P.2.3

1 Originally, the global luxury industry moved only from west to east.
2 Traditionally, long-established brands were the most popular.
3 In recent times, there have been global changes.
4 Now, more and more Asian brands are appearing in American shops.
5 Nowadays, France is the top destination for wealthy Chinese shoppers.
6 In the future, Asian brands may be as popular as Western ones.
7 Twenty years ago, nobody would have expected these developments.
8 Twenty years from now, the situation may have changed beyond recognition.

3.1 Stress in derived words

🔊 P.3.1

1 Commitment is a so-called soft skill.
2 Job-seekers face a lot of competition.
3 What does the expression 'come across well' mean?
4 We're looking for a Key Account Manager.
5 How would you describe your personality?
6 Would you apply for a job if you didn't have the necessary qualifications?
7 Willingness to travel is a key requirement.
8 Have you ever applied for an internship?
9 I've written five job applications this week.
10 Her résumé is impressive.

3.2 Voice range and intonation in indirect questions

🔊 P.3.2

1 Can you tell me something about your previous experience?
2 I'd like to know whether you'd be prepared to work overtime.
3 Could you tell me what your greatest passion is?
4 I'd be interested to know something about your computer skills.
5 Can you give me some more details about your previous job?
6 Could you say if you'd be willing to do some training?
7 I'd like to know when you'd be able to start?
8 Could you explain why you decided to leave your previous job?

4.3 /iː/, /ɪ/, /eɪ/ and /aɪ/

🔊 P.4.1

1 feel
2 eight
3 try
4 delay
5 right
6 lead
7 late
8 list
9 wait
10 fill
11 green
12 limit
13 deal
14 raise
15 still
16 style
17 white
18 decide
19 straight
20 street

4.4 Intonation in 'OK'

🔊 P.4.2

1 [showing that you understand and agree – fall–rise intonation] OK
2 [falling intonation at end – trying to get people's attention] OK
3 [showing that you understand what someone says but you don't necessarily agree – slow, long drawn-out fall–rise] OK
4 [rising intonation at the end – asking someone to agree with you] OK?

🔊 P.4.3

1 [falling intonation at end – trying to get people's attention] OK, can I have everyone's attention, please?
2 [rising intonation at the end – asking someone to agree with you] I think it's time for a break. OK?
3 [showing that you understand and agree – fall–rise intonation] OK, that's fine by me.
4 [showing that you understand what someone says but you don't necessarily agree – slow, long drawn-out fall–rise] OK, I see what you mean, but I'm not sure I really agree.
5 [showing that you understand and agree – fall–rise intonation] OK, that's perfect.
6 [falling intonation at end – trying to get people's attention] OK, let's get down to business.
7 [showing that you understand what someone says but you don't necessarily agree – slow, long drawn-out fall–rise] OK, I'll need to think about that.
8 [rising intonation at the end – asking someone to agree with you] Let's meet at two o'clock, OK?

5.1 Pausing and stress in presentations

🔊 P.5.1

With the orders packed, | they are ready to leave the warehouse | and begin the next stage in the process | – delivery to the customer. | Delivery can be undertaken by the postal service | or by courier companies. | Frequently, | customers are able to track the progress of their package online. | Consumers enjoy the convenience of having goods delivered to their homes. | Of course, | customers are not always at home to receive their package. |

One solution is to use these: | they are called collection lockers. | Packages can be left inside | and the customer can pick them up at any time | by entering a PIN number. |

The logistics that e-commerce relies upon | are developing all the time. | In the future, | we may see some changes in the way our online shopping is delivered. |

This robot | has been designed to deliver packages. | Customers can arrange to collect their goods from the robot | via a mobile app. | Some companies | are also considering using drones to transport goods to customers.

5.2 Auxiliary verbs in passives

🔊 P.5.2

1 Logistics can be defined as the business of transporting things to the place where they're needed.
2 The advertisement's been viewed 85 million times.
3 A self-driving lorry's already been designed.
4 Drivers'll be given new tasks.
5 The driver'll be able to get out of the truck and rest while it's unloaded and loaded.
6 Drivers aren't going to be made completely redundant.
7 This robot's been designed to deliver packages.
8 When the orders have been packed, they're delivered to the customer.

🔊 P.5.3

1 The advertisement with the splits stunt was made to demonstrate the effectiveness of the steering system.
2 Self-driving systems for lorries and buses have been developed.
3 Drivers aren't going to be made completely redundant.
4 This robot's been designed to deliver packages.
5 Experiments are being conducted with drones.
6 When the orders have been packed, they're delivered to the customer.
7 Goods can be collected from the robot via a mobile app.
8 Logistics can be defined as the business of transporting things to the place where they're needed.

6.1 Consonant–vowel linking

🔊 P.6.1

1 at the top_of the building
2 linked_in to the system
3 it lasts_a week_or two
4 this is the fourth_attempt
5 do you feel_OK?
6 more than seven_hours later
7 set_off_an alarm
8 watch_all the programmes

🔊 P.6.2

1 Under what circumstances would you start_a business?
2 What would be the right kind_of business for you?
3 What_are the three biggest_ attractions and disadvantages_of running your_own business?
4 The amount_of business done_ over_a period_of time_is called turnover.
5 Demand_is the need_or desire that people have for particular goods_ and services.
6 What_are some_of the difficulties_ of the fast growth_of a start-up like Fairphone?
7 A business angel_is someone who gives_a business money, often_in exchange for_a share of the company.
8 What types_of consumers might be interested_in buying your products_or services?
9 The company reduces_its impact_ on the environment by recycling minerals.
10 Which_of the business_ideas would you invest_in?

6.4 Intonation and discourse marking in presentations

🔊 P.6.3

1 This morning, | I'd like to give you a quick update on the progress we've made so far.
2 If you look at this bar chart, | you can see how the markets compare.
3 These figures | give a clear indication of how sales have grown.
4 On this slide | you can see a summary of what I've told you so far.
5 Next, | let's move on to customer age demographics.
6 What's especially interesting in this chart | is the left-hand column.
7 I'd like to finish | by showing you a forecast for the next six months.
8 If you have any questions, | I'll be very happy to answer them.

7.2 Phrasing and intonation in past sentences

🔊 P.7.1

1 Things were going well in 2007, which is when Pawel moved to the States.
2 But he'd only been there a year when the economic crisis happened.
3 It was the first time he'd lived abroad, and he immediately noticed lots of small differences.
4 When he was talking to people, he realised that communication was much faster.
5 While he was walking to the office, he saw sidewalks that suddenly ended in the middle of nowhere.
6 He'd never seen anything like that before, so he was pretty surprised.
7 He hadn't worked for a global corporation before, and he found the style of communication rather different.
8 Because he hadn't been to the States before, he wasn't used to distances being measured in minutes.

7.3 Strong or weak?

🔊 P.7.2

1 As for me
2 I think the process is important
3 but not as important as the result
4 If the group can't reach a decision
5 the person responsible has to make one
6 Deadlines can be moved around
7 but only if they really have to be
8 I think once decisions have been made
9 you should respect them
10 even if you don't agree with them

🔊 P.7.3

1 As for me, I think the process is important, yes, but not as important as the result.
2 If the group can't reach a decision, the person responsible has to make one.
3 Deadlines can be moved around, but only if they really have to be.
4 I think once decisions have been made, you should respect them, even if you don't agree with them.
5 It's good to reach a consensus if you can, but it isn't always possible.
6 If you want to be perceived as competent, you should respect deadlines.
7 Decisiveness is even more important than consensus.
8 You should act as a group, even if there are disagreements in the group.

8.1 Glottal stops

🔊 P.8.1

1 I can't understand. (t)
2 I've got to go. (glottal stop)
3 I've got an idea. (t)
4 What are you wearing? (glottal stop)
5 There's a lot going on. (glottal stop)
6 Sit on the floor. (t)
7 Wait for me. (glottal stop)
8 Let me help. (glottal stop)

🔊 P.8.2

1 Just got a taste of what it's like to be in charge.
2 To what extent is it entertainment and to what extent is it educational?
3 A good manager knows when to delegate jobs.
4 The new manager is finding it hard to win his staff's respect.

5 Making tough decisions is an essential part of leadership.
6 Staff aren't going to trust you if you don't care what they think.
7 I'm not sure you're right this time.
8 In what ways can a manager set an example for the team?

8.2 Phrasing and intonation in relative clauses

 P.8.3

1 The meeting, which was scheduled to start at 10 o'clock, was delayed by half an hour.

2 The room where the meeting was due to be held hadn't been cleaned and prepared.
3 We need staff who can adapt to changing circumstances.
4 My friend and colleague, who works in the next office, is away on a training course.
5 One of the managers, who has worked here for over 30 years, is retiring next month.
6 Is it possible for people who have a fixed mindset to change how they think?

7 Abbie Smith, who works at Chicago Booth Business School, has looked at the benefits for companies that appoint 'frugal' executives.
8 Entrepreneurs, who are less afraid of risks than managers, are better at taking 'hot' decisions.
9 What are the five key elements which are required to develop neuroleadership skills?
10 A new book, which has the title *Neuroscience for Leadership*, points out the need for years of practice, reflection and feedback.